LEAN INTO DELUSION

LEAN INTO DELUSION

Free Your Mind Through Trusting Your Intuition

DANIELLE CHYLINSKI

chylinski media

chylinskimedia.com | @chylinskimedia

Chylinski Media

Lean Into Delusion

Copyright © 2023 by Danielle Chylinski
Published by Chylinski Media

Print ISBN 979-8-9875568-2-5 (hardcover)

Visit chylinskimedia.com for more information about the author and updates.

First Printing, 2023

To my boyfriend, Alex, for loving & supporting me
through a chaotic 2+ years of writing this book;

To our dog, Oliver, for being a true therapy dog when I need him most;

To my brother, Jeffrey, for holding a similar philosophy of life,
allowing me to never feel alone in this world;

To my Dad, George, for reminding me
I'm more like you than I'll ever know;

To my Mom, Lynn, for inspiring me to be the exact person I am today;

Thank you. *This book exists because of you.*

CONTENTS

A Note From the Author

"So frustrating when I share a high about my day with someone and their response is, 'That's not reality.'"

"Wait, how old are you?" my brother asked. "Thirty-seven?"

"Twenty-seven," I laughed.

His eyes lit up like, *Oh shit.*

We've *always* been two years apart, but he did a double take.

"You're constantly reminding me what we can accomplish without an age attached to the accomplishment. It's wild," he said back to me.

Really? It's all about reflecting inward and asking yourself, "What am I choosing to accomplish when I'm not tying myself down to societal standards, such as, how old should I be or what degrees I should have earned to achieve some goal?"

Not everyone will understand your non-traditional choices and growth.

Things get awkward when someone asks for your age or what year you graduated from high school or college (assuming you went), especially when you can tell they're trying to mentally place you in some arbitrary societal box based on the information they gather. Subconsciously, the person asking the questions often has preconceived thoughts about who you are, what you've accomplished, and what you're capable of based solely on the number of years you've been alive.

Hmmm, I thought to myself. *I usually forget about my age until someone else mentions it.*

My brother and I both learned you're *supposed to* graduate from college in your early twenties... but then what? Well, at that point, the timeline of your future is, *finally*, for you to decide.

How can we unlearn what we expect from a "steady" job, an "ideal" living situation, a "necessary" relationship status and all the other real-world experiences that fall along the path of success leading up to the age of thirty?

Regardless of your age, you will adapt to your chosen environment.

As a person in her twenties, people have told me:

"You have so many years ahead of you. Slow down."

"You're young. Take a deep breath. You have time."

"At your age, I..."

"Don't burn yourself out."

"Oh my gosh, you're *only* 22? If *only* I could do what you're doing now!"

Fuck. So exhausting to hear.

While some of these comments made me question my choices and my jam-packed way of living, they also encouraged me. Still, at times I get this weird feeling of guilt when I *actually accomplish something* because in the back of my mind, I remember negative comments about my youth and would often second-guess myself.

For me, staying engaged in various activities has kept me completely on task with my desires, which is the way I've grown to live my life. Fully planning my day with little wiggle room for years, to me, meant I had little time to pause, overthink, or debate whether I was doing was the right or wrong thing.

For some people, having the highest level of formal education as possible to earn a higher salary is crucial. Others know they don't need or want formal post-secondary education to build *their* dream life. And then there are others who default to continuing their education because they're unsure of what they want or unsure of the path they've chosen.

They shrug and think they've figured out a clever way to delay the *real world*—whether personal or professional.

What we often forget is that the *real world* begins when you decide it does.

Stop allowing others' opinions or words to delay that privilege for you. You're not delaying anything except *your own* happiness.

I can remember a time before I was aware of my control over shaping my reality, where I let society into the driver's seat. Ever since I learned how insurance works (I mean, still sort of learning but), I've thought about turning twenty-six—the age where my parents' insurance plan would no longer cover me. I thought; *damn, I'll have my own plan, which means I need to have a job with a solid plan. Either that, or get married and hop on his!* It was then when I felt like I was on a fast track to growing up and being *an adult.*

This arbitrary institutional event was affecting me so deeply that, at one point, I told myself when I turned twenty-five, I was going to quit my job and *do crazy shit*—the definition of crazy shit at this point was TBD. I was planning one last adventure before having to get a "real job" that provided insurance. *Imagine tha*t. Well, I imagined this scenario enough to where I made it my reality.

I quit my full-time, secure, benefit-paying job in July 2021, a few weeks before I turned 26. I found my clarity. *Let's not live life based on needing insurance funded by someone else, Danielle, LOL.*

Twenty-five-year-old Danielle realized; *I could be me on my time, with my own expectations. Every day is my day.*

To be respected and professional in someone else's environment is one thing, but to embody the confidence to successfully and efficiently do it on my own is another.

Okay, real talk though... I realized clarity did not exactly exist in the moment. I *finally* was in a position where I was about to go on an insurance plan through a great company, and in the moment, I *chose to* walk away and attempt to figure out how to get *my own plan.*

NOW, choosing to work for myself meant choosing to be myself 24/7/365 with no conditions.

In deciding to work for myself and to be a millennial woman in business, I went against what others expected based on societal standards, and honestly, what I expected of myself. Growing up, I didn't know you could get an insurance plan if you didn't work for a company. And once I realized my own plan was an option, I thought insurance would be thousands of dollars based on what *everyone* around me made it seem like. (It's not.)

Historically, I had *chosen to* follow other people's standards to keep me safe and sane, but I've viewed them as a tool rather than a blueprint. Consistently taking what I'm "supposed to do" as recommendations as opposed to strict guidelines has naturally always been my vibe. I appreciate recommendations, but ultimately, I consider what other people suggest, and then I follow my intuition.

Over the last few years, it's been increasingly apparent how damaging, frustrating, and uncomfortable blindly complying with societal standards can be. I've documented these relations in connection to my life on social media, which have given us the power, leverage and opportunity to share our stories and experiences.

For years I've found myself saying yes to sharing my story, taking time and creating space to do a deep dive into what happened (or what didn't) and why. The vulnerability I allowed for myself, by myself, gave me the strength for consistent, deep reflection; this made me want to share my experiences even more. All of my raw stories may not be easy to share in the moment, but eventually, I find I *do* want to share the ins and outs of my life, including the "embarrassing" or times when I've felt guilty or even ashamed.

For me, there are no secrets: like not doing any research on a job or industry before accepting the offer, taking a 20K pay cut or having no choice but to be strong in a courtroom month after month because the guy I thought was going to be "the strong one," couldn't be. I've been open about how people or experiences have affected me, like attending college with my major as *undecided* because I had no fucking clue who I was, or how I purposely avoided all math and anything business related because I *knew* I'd never have a business role; yet, now, I've owned a business for over three years.

After sharing my own vulnerable stories, I soon learned many people fear sharing experiences and making space to meet *their own* vulnerability. They often say, "I don't need people knowing my business." But here's a question to ask yourself: Do you need them *not* to know *that thing* about you, or are you afraid of how you'll feel when you share *that truth* about yourself?

For me, being open about my experience on this Earth has been what keeps me, me. I enjoy being open and sharing all aspects of my reality. It's human. We, as a society, focus *so much* on outcomes, and don't talk enough about the process. I love sharing with others how parts of my life came to fruition, or didn't, because too often our failures and successes look like they happened overnight.

I want you to see the value in what sharing experiences can do for you and those around you.

Sharing my journey as it happens eliminates the idea of focusing solely on the outcomes and not the process, in my mind.

I choose to be vulnerable instead of worrying about what *might* happen if I share *too much* about myself. Sharing feels so free. Nothing to hide, nothing to be embarrassed about. I want to be comfortable in what I cannot control versus striving for perfection. I continue to recognize and honor my feelings instead of trying to be someone I think other people feel I should be.

It doesn't feel good when the weight of someone else's opinions of what you should or shouldn't do is on your shoulders every second of each day.

We're not meant to prioritize someone else's expectation of what our life should look, be, and feel like.

That's why I wrote this book; I've accepted my reality is my reality, and it differs from others, the same way your reality is your own and does not match anyone else's. Accepting my reality has been a survival tool for me, like I saved myself without realizing before I fell too deep off the edge. The more conversations I have, the more I've learned we're all just looking for someone to stick their hand out and help make our journey a little easier.

While some would rather not disturb the peace, living with countless negative thoughts in their head, I choose to be vocal and address them directly in the moment. I've grown to be fantastic at cutting people off and walking away from things that don't serve me. And for some people that's harsh, but that's what I have discovered is healthiest for me. There are too many people in the world to spend time convincing someone why you feel they should love and support you. I've come to understand that if people have a hard time wrapping their head around my reality, where I make the rules, it's not my problem.

I want you to feel the same way.

Recently, one of my friends told me no one thinks about your life more than you do. People can give their input, share their experiences, say whatever they want, but at the end of the day, only *you* know how you feel.

We all already have our own philosophy for living; we just need to break down and analyze our philosophy more often. By sharing it, we can recognize how we go through similar experiences, emotions, and traumas that shape us into who we are.

I hope, besides getting to know me and my philosophy, this book will help you understand and embrace *your own* philosophy of life.

I'm finally in a place where I'm ready to share more concretely what I've learned about myself over the last twenty-five years, with a focus on the last ten years when I created and established my professional life and my business, Chylinski Media.

I make the rules around who I choose to spend time with, how I choose to spend that time, what I choose to say, how I react to certain situations, what boundaries I set and hold, and who I choose to be.

I'm happy in my skin, with my flaws, with the highs and lows of my journey, and how I decide to live.

We achieve happiness not through steps people tell us to take, but through the steps in life you choose to take.

Do you ever think about meeting the person you could have been? *The person who didn't; take the risk, send the email, make the phone call, post the video, make the tough decisions, choose what was best for themselves over everything.*

The answers are within you. You just need to let them out.

Not everything said in this book will be for everyone, just like not every TV show you start on Netflix is for you. You may think, *love this* or *fuck this* while reading. Take what you need and leave what you don't. If it's not for you, pass it onto someone else who may like it, need it, or benefit from it. You need to do what you need to do for yourself to be at peace.

By continuing to share my stories, I hope it inspires you to share yours. Telling these stories out loud and remembering the power of conversation can teach and remind us of the person we're meant to be.

But for now, close your eyes, visualize the life you want to live, turn the page confidently, and *lean into delusion*.

P.S. Names shared are pseudonyms, aside from family and companies.

Parts Summarized

Learning, Unlearning, Repeat
The sooner you realize you're constantly navigating between
past expectations and your current reality, the more you
can own your narrative, feelings, & decision making.

Recognizing External Influence
When you're feeling uncomfortable and the negative self-talk creeps
in, it's easier to get in your own way than out. You may talk
yourself into what you think something will be prior to allowing
the experience to happen, then make a judgment about it.
Sometimes life seems *so hard*, when in reality, it has a lot
to do with unlearning what you thought was *normal*.

Self Awareness
Surround yourself with people who align with what you *actually*
want. Be willing to create change when you intuitively feel
the need, even though it will cause resistance. Talking about
reality negatively will always keep you in a miserable state,
so what's possible when you change your narrative?

Expectations

Learning how to manage your expectations of others can help you better understand what is stopping or distracting you from prioritizing yourself. You may often put others' needs before your own—why?

Confidence Check

As a human, you have a constant need to feel significant but also a fear of being seen. Conformity is easy because it's comfortable and there's *minimum* risk. Lack of confidence comes from trying to be something you're innately not. Understand the responsibility you have in life to express and embrace confidence to thrive as an individual.

You Decide

Seems *obvious*, right? *It is.* How you choose to represent yourself directly aligns with what you'll attract into your presence. Remain aware of what is and is not working in your decision-making process, putting into perspective what changes you can implement daily.

Introduction: Shut the Fuck Up & Be You

My apartment was filled with frantic energy. *Is today an eye shadow or no eye shadow day? I want to change this song but I also need to get my hair curled like 10 minutes ago. Did I miss a piece in the back or not? I didn't even think about getting my nails done. Fuck. I'm so happy I spent the last two years donating clothes from my closet that didn't feel* **me**. *That's saving minutes, maybe hours, on getting ready. Okay, wait, I'm sweating. It's fine. I have like 2 more strands to curl. I wish I could put my hair in a messy bun. Ugh. Actually, should I?*

Brand shoots seemed like something too out-of-reach for someone like me—*too* professional, *too* posed, *too* fake, and *too* put together. Yet, here I am. They bring me right back to high school picture days; wake up at 6 a.m., mentally prepare to look flawless all day, then have your picture taken around 1 p.m. during period 6. Yup, I became triggered by this weird, deeply rooted delusion that when someone has a *legit* camera, you get *ready ready*.

You're no longer simply impressing yourself; You're trying to impress others.

When I imagined a brand shoot, I used to envision being told what to do: how to pose, how to smile, how to tilt my head... all things I wouldn't naturally do. However, part of me knew that one day I would find the perfect person behind the lens who took the time to understand me for, well, *me*. I wanted someone who would embrace me, as I am, instead of trying to capture their perception of "perfect" me.

The phone rang, interrupting my mid-day dream.

I picked up. "I'm here," said Cara, the photographer.

Ah, fuck.

I got in the elevator, ran to my car to grab my makeup bag, met her in the lobby and raced us back upstairs. Sweating, uncomfortable, but trying to act cool, I held the door to my apartment open as Cara carried in all of her equipment. I raced past her to the bathroom to finish getting ready.

"Come on in here! I'm almost done." I said, out of breath.

With a big smile on Cara's face, "Danielle, I'm so pumped for this brand photoshoot. What are you wearing today?"

"You can look in my closet and grab whatever you think will look the best on me," I said to Cara.

She looked at me confused, like, *why would this girl not have over prepared to feel and look her best?*

"But it's *your* shoot," she said. "So *you* tell me what *you* want to wear!"

"I love *every* piece of clothing in my closet, so seriously, pick whatever *you* think will photograph best. *I will feel myself regardless.*"

While Cara was pulling outfits from the closet, she asked, "Out of curiosity, what's your go-to response when someone asks what you do?"

"Great question. *LOL.* I honestly don't know anymore. Recently, I've been consciously inconsistent in posting on social media so no new business inquiries come in."

"WHAT? Why don't you want more business? I wish I had that problem," she said back to me.

"I've realized I don't want to *just* attract business; I want to attract the right business, the right people, the right opportunities for *me.* I've been showing up consistently online for 10 years, so the connections I've made throughout that time understand me for *me.* They know what to expect and how I operate. And if someone is new to the party, they can look at my past posts and get to know me quickly. So now, my posts are more a reminder like, *Hi, I still exist. Here's what I'm up to. Here's what I'm thinking about...* and less of me *trying to* prove anything: my worth, skill set, credibility. In this new season I've entered, I'm evolving and finding clarity around myself as Danielle Chylinski. I fill my days with reflecting, dreaming, and analyzing the life I'm living and the life I'm building. I have learned growth is in the *being* rather than the *doing* and *proving*."

"Damn. I want to get there. I'm afraid to even talk about my business out loud, never mind social media because I feel like I don't even know what to say."

"Exactly. Once you're in a conversation and mention you have a business, you get hit with the... *OMG, how cool. I wish I could have my own business. How do you like it? I wish I could quit my job. Who are your clients? How did you decide to start the business?* You usually don't even get to say what you *actually* do and the impact you're out to create because you get slammed with a million and twelve questions."

"YES!" Cara agreed. "I feel like I do much more than what I'm able to tell someone. When people hear I'm a photographer, they instantly make an assumption about me. If I don't have the chance to explain my approach or the art I'm creating, I could miss an opportunity."

"Same girl. When a marketing outsider hears me mention social media, their brain goes directly to managing accounts for other people. But I do *so much more* than that. I enjoy helping people embody and understand a brand fully, identity included, rather than just telling them what their brand *needs* to do *to be successful*."

"Definitely," Cara said. "And I want to ask you a million questions, but I don't want to box you in, so I hold back."

I totally get it, I thought to myself. *I want to switch the conversation to, "Okay, enough about me. How are you? How can I help and encourage you to be more you? What support do you need to show up online like you do in person?" I want others to get extreme value out of their interactions with me; I don't want to only be a small burst of inspo. I'm not here to help people be me. I'm here to help people be them.*

"It's easy to ask someone about their life and get inspired, but it's not always easy to turn inspiration into motivation or action," I replied to Cara. "I want to impact someone like you immediately in the moment so you can walk away from the conversation feeling empowered to make your own rules, without second guessing. It's easy to get overwhelmed at the thought of your personal brand, but I want to talk about the hard stuff. What are you constantly telling yourself you can't do? Why do you feel you're not worthy of a goal you have?"

Cara stayed focused. "Mmmmmm."

"Seriously though, Cara, *what keeps you up at night?*"

Did that question make you uncomfortable? Did you answer it in your head or skip it and keep reading? We rarely ask ourselves or get asked the tough questions.

"So true," she said back.

"I want to remind you, and others, that your personal brand is not another thing to add to your to-do list. You're not necessarily *building* something. You're not *working* towards something. You're being something; you're being you. It shouldn't feel like work because you're showing up *fully and only* as you are. The second it does, it's no longer authentic. And sometimes, I *only* have a few minutes, or even seconds, to get my point across. I need to be better at sharing those thoughts versus hoping I get the opportunity to."

Personal branding has become another way of saying be aware of your identity, share and own who you are in all aspects of your life.

Cara grabbed four pairs of pants, a ton of shirts, and a few pairs of shoes. I grabbed my desktop computer, a bag filled with little fake plants and notebooks, and my boyfriend carried my desk up to our rooftop.

After shooting around for fifteen minutes, I looked at Cara and said, "Okay, what else?"

"Let's see the signature *Danielle messy bun*. I want to get a cute shot with your bun peeking over your computer screen," Cara smiled.

Fuck, do a perfect messy bun on the spot? To be photographed in like .5 seconds, no mirror, only the reflection from my computer screen. Yeah, sure, I can definitely NOT do that, but okay, give me a sec. I can do it.

Less than a minute later, a bun was up and she was serving paparazzi vibes. My curled hair I rushed (while sweating) to perfect for this shoot was now *destroyed*.

I've accepted my reality is just that: *mine.* Just like yours is *only* yours. If people have a hard time understanding your reality, where you're in complete control, that's not your problem to unpack.

"You should be more confident," they say. But, then when you exude confidence, the narrative switches.

"She's so full of herself. Do you see her? She's way too confident. It's embarrassing."

How are we, especially as women, expected to be *more* confident, but not *too* confident? Where is the imaginary line we are not supposed to cross where people start criticizing us for embracing who we are, where we excel and what we love?

This isn't another how-to book.

I'm not here to tell you what to think or what to do. I'm only saying things I think are worth sharing, hoping to create a space that allows your mind to wander to where it **needs** to go.

I think people often read books because they're searching for someone to tell them *exactly what* to do so they can, in turn, follow the exact steps and experience the promised results.

I, however, want you to *actually* think for yourself.

We're so used to others telling us what to do that we no longer trust what *our actual body* is telling us. When we feel stagnant, it's usually because we're not listening to ourselves... we're quieting our own intelligence in favor of others' opinions.

We need to understand *who we actually are*—not who Mom or Dad told you to be, not how your teachers expected you to act, not what society makes you feel you need to do. Rather, *who are you when you, and only you, decide*?

Although we may think the journey of understanding who we are should be done alone, in silence, or behind closed doors, the most effective way to understand yourself is through sharing the journey; allowing people to follow no matter where you are in it.

Through stories, you will see the importance of sharing your experiences rather than hiding them, and the power of putting your words and thoughts into existence.

You'll learn the importance of connecting with yourself first, before seeking validation from others.

You'll understand the significance of how being present creates a life of attraction instead of a life of defense.

You'll experience how *everything* naturally falls into place when you value yourself—*your true self.*

When it comes to social media, each business has their own strategy or method to *get you results.*

Here's the catch: when you get to the root of it all, the advice starts to sound the same.

"Post (insert number) times a day. Use (insert hashtags) to increase your reach. Post at (insert time of day) for the most visibility."

The structure and lack of flexibility and customization becomes overwhelming and confusing, not to mention, always changing. So, how do *you* succeed under these conditions?

We rarely consider, out of all the decisions we make, how many of our decisions are *our own* versus what someone else told us we *should do*?

Anyone can tell you what to do, but hearing other people's stories, genuine real life experiences, combined with reflecting on your own lived experience, will lead you towards making decisions that are best for you.

You are everything you need.

I have written this book hoping the stories and reflections shared throughout help you to find the clarity you need. And by that I mean what *you actually* need—not what *I tell* you *you need.*

If you've read this far (and didn't skip the intro like I normally do when I read books, whoops) and are determined to go further, then **let's fucking get into it.**

Learning, Unlearning, Repeat

The sooner you realize you're constantly navigating between past expectations and your current reality, the more you can own your narrative, feelings, & decision making.

1. Intuition-Based Living

"Danielle, I can't believe how much you talk now. You were so shy growing up."

Key word: growing up.

Growing up, and well into my early twenties, *they* saw me as the "good girl," the quiet girl. Now, only a few years later, a perception of me may be radically different. I now realize I wasn't shy; I'm not shy. I just often find myself in a mental space where I don't want to contribute to the noise. I've always wanted to contribute with logic, reason, and experience.

Reflecting on my past with this newfound realization has brought immense clarity.

When I felt hurt by someone around me, I would shut down, no longer having anything to say. I remember a time in middle school where I went days without talking. It gets exhausting: constant drama, lies, targeted deceit, hurtful words and actions by people you trust.

People make perceptions about your reality in an effort to make them feel better about themselves.

Oh yeah, and I swear a fuck ton. Sorry, not sorry.

So, now that I got that off my chest, hi!

I'm Danielle. Danielle Lynn Chylinski, if you want to get personal (I do). My mom's first name is Lynn. While we're here, my brother's name is Jeffrey George Chylinski, after my dad, George. Can you imagine how that conversation went?

"So, what should Danielle's middle name be?"

"I think it should be mine."

"I agree."

2 years later, Jeffrey is born.

"So . . . Jeffrey's middle name should *obviously* be my name, right?"

"Right."

Born in '95, I grew up in Connecticut during a time where we didn't have access to social media like we do now. Not proud to say I got in trouble for creating a MySpace account behind my parents' back, but yeah, I'm *kind of a badass.* As if making the account without permission wasn't bad enough, my dad made me delete my entire account because my profile picture was inappropriate—Me, in a Hollister tank top & shorts, holding my 2x4 digital camera, white with pink polka dots, up in the mirror with one hand, and throwing up the peace sign with the other.

Looking back, I was innocent and naïve until I went to college. I had no idea other people live their lives in such extremely different ways. I thought *everyone* in the world knew about Connecticut—where it's located, how the seasons change, how each town varies with stigma, socioeconomic classes, and levels of education. I didn't even understand the idea that each state has their own set of vibes—lots of vibes. *Holy fuck.* How does anyone keep track?

Growing up, I didn't know what questions to even ask in order to widen my perspective. Those who were in a position to guide me were showing me a black and white world, one in which I didn't fit into.

So, I followed the guidance of those around me at the lunch table.

What did you do?

No one was talking about our future after high school. It seemed like all that mattered was if I could be the one to drive the group (illegally, since I hadn't had my license for a full year yet, like Connecticut required) to the mall in my car. No one was talking about what colleges seemed to align best with who we were and who we wanted to be. Apparently, our clothing or what boys thought of us mattered more.

You hear about how people's stories are all different when you're younger. Yet, you don't feel much different from the person next to you because you're all following the same path: preschool, elementary school, middle school, high school, college.

This was during the "I post Facebook photo albums with 20+ photos *every* time I leave the house," and "I share random depressing song quotes to low-key call out certain people who are supposed to be my friend," era.

Can you picture the college fairs your high school would host? And the military guys who would set up a 6x6 plastic table in the cafeteria during lunch and try to recruit you? In my little town, it seemed like those two things (college and the military) were the *only* options for students after they graduated. Trade schools were rarely mentioned, but when they were, they were for the "others"...those who "weren't smart enough" or "couldn't afford" college. Starting a business? Never heard of it.

When I was a junior in high school, I didn't even know what a GPA was. Not being dramatic; I'm serious. Once I learned about GPAs and why they mattered, I discovered my high school GPA was under a 3.0.

The fuck.

I was confused (and embarrassed) because I was culturally taught not to bring attention to your GPA if it's under a 3.0.

"You'll never get into college," they would say, or "The closer to 4.0, the better off you are." This all contributed to my perceived shyness. I was often seen as an "us" while feeling like a "them." So, I wouldn't speak up. I often kept my inner experience bottled up so I could fit in.

Despite completing the homework *every classmate* wanted to copy, all the attempts to cheat off of me during tests, being the girl people would want to partner with assuming she'd do the majority of the project, and the one people would call late at night to borrow her book, hoping there was hand-written notes in it, I was a *less than 3.0* student. When I realized, I felt divided between what adults were telling me I *should* be versus how my peers were treating me.

Now looking back, I realized *your worth* externally is all perception. GPA is only a number based on how professors graded your performance based on a systematic scale. I didn't fit their scale to be over a 3.0, but I fit the over 3.0 scale to my peers.

Why? How?

Did you grow up thinking your GPA represented your worth?

What did it mean if I committed to a college where I was *below average* according to my GPA? What did it mean if I committed to a college where I was *above average*? Was I confident enough to commit to a school that basically told me I was *only average*?

Beliefs trigger reactions.

Once my belief switched from, "I need over a 3.0 GPA to get into college," to "I'm good enough for college," I felt confident touring college campuses and putting myself in the shoes of a potential fresh-man. The ability to envision myself in college came from an important realization: My worth came from being the person I wanted to be, and my college experience would later be a reflection of my new belief.

My experience of applying for college was awkward. I literally asked my guidance counselor, who knew nothing about me besides the occasional random mini meltdown I'd have in his office, which colleges I *should* apply to. Side note, my meltdowns usually consisted of, "Why do I need to take math classes? What even are actual friends? How come I need to spend time studying when I *should* be learning enough in class?"

My counselor gave me a *blueprint* of where to visit, but it was up to me to decide from there. I ended up committing to a private school with about 2,500 undergrad students in Springfield, Massachusetts, even though I spent my entire childhood counting down the days I could leave the Northeast and go somewhere where no one could real-istically ever visit me. But yeah, instead I went a mere 45-minute drive away from my parent's house.

Once I toured the campus with my mom, I felt like it was exactly where I needed to be—every kid on campus was smiling, holding the door open for you without thinking, and the dining hall had a big ass salad bar.

Yes, your GPA predetermines which schools you can get into, but it has no impact on your college experience once you're there. Once you're in, you're in. Who you are when you're there is on you.

The way people acted towards me directly resulted from how I handled and showed up for myself daily, not because they knew what was on my transcript.

I entered college with my major as "Undecided" because I literally was undecided. I mean, how would I have *actually* decided if I *just* learned what GPA meant 405 days before I started college? Don't fact check me on that number, though. Point is, that's enough days to make it apparent I was not ready to declare what I would do in the future.

Meanwhile, I listened to my friends talk about how they chose a major, yet were extremely anxious and unsure if they'd stay committed to their choice. They'd talk constantly about the options if they decided to change, listing all the pros and cons. It all sounded like nothing I wanted to be involved in, so unlike my friends, I didn't allow the pressure of deciding put me in a box. I committed to and was proud to be undecided.

... at first.

You should have seen the looks on adults' faces when they asked me what I *decided* my college major to be.

conversation on repeat

"*Undecided*? You don't have any idea? Like at all?"

"I just don't want to do math."

end conversation

I went into college lost about who I was and what I was good at. Growing up, my mom frequently told me, "Be average at *everything*: school, sports and social life." I was happy to be in college, but not for the right reasons.

I was happy because I was still on the path doing what adults told me was *the right thing to do*—get your degree. I was spending all of this money to attend a University even though I had a you *should* go to trade school *GPA*, according to my Connecticut peeps.

The *only* thing I had decided was to get involved in clubs (college clubs, not like fun bar clubs). Embracing my *inner nerd* made my *cool friends* uncomfortable. Regardless, I knew I wanted to be an active member in the campus community. I often thought to myself, *How do I want to spend my time outside of class? Who could I meet and how could I learn from them and their experience?*

Later I learned *this is networking*. Can you believe it? I knew how to network before I was told by *every* single adult at *every* single important function, "If you want to be successful, you must network."

Networking is one of those things where we're told how important it is, but I think people continue to overthink it. All networking *really means* is to have conversations, build relationships and maintain them. It's so simple that it's hard for many to wrap their head around.

"You mean I just have to talk to people like they're people?" Yes.

While who you know is important, it's also about how you know them and the connection you have with them. You never know how each connection will play out.

After talking to random people in the lunch line, starting a conversation with a classmate sitting next to me, and many more, "Sup stranger, I'm Danielle. Who are you?" interactions, I started making decisions. I was accepted as a member of the Class of 2017 Class Council, which hosted events for students to enjoy each other's company, marketed campus-wide. I joined Student Senate (which I later learned is basically set up like the real Senate and your first name doesn't matter... you instantly become Senator *insert last name*). As Senator Chylinski—Freshman Representative, later earning the title of Publicity Chair—this was the first role I held in college which fell under the PR/Marketing/Social bubble I now fully align and identify with. The year after, my classmates elected me as Sophomore Representative, then Secretary. SO MANY TITLES, right? Yuck.

Next, something weird happened.

After all the "We need you Danielle," and "You have to run for President; there is no one else who makes sense but you," comments, I said YOLO and ran for President... *President of Student Senate.* President of the 2,500+ undergrad students at the University. I hit this delusional state. I felt a strong pull to keep moving forward.

Being elected was such an out-of-body experience because I was like, "WTF, is this my actual reality?" and my brain was like, "Mhhh-mmmm."

Looking back, I realize I got into college, not confidently, but confused. I went in lost about what I was good at, and by the end of my sophomore year I felt hopeless about being major-less. That's when I met with my career counselor, Sarah—a strong, confident woman with an underlying intensity to help students figure out what they're meant to do.

"I'm in all these clubs and hold various positions," I told Sarah. "Somehow I *always* end up helping with social media things, creating flyers or putting together bulletin boards. The wind blew away my cut-out letters and pictures the other day while I designed a few bulletin boards outside. I chased them around and people would stare at me or help me chase them. I don't get how I can do all these things around campus and help other people, yet still feel extremely lost about the actual direction of my college education."

Sarah was staring back at me with an odd look, but kinda smirky. "Danielle, what you're doing sounds like a Communication major with a concentration in Public Relations. This major would be a perfect fit for you."

I couldn't have said "SIGN ME UP" quick enough.

Walking out of Sarah's office with confidence, I held my head high like, *who the fuck can I tell that I finally figured out my major? Hell yeah. Go me!*

Then, I bumped into a new friend, Trev, and he stopped to chat. After a few minutes of small talk, he asked what my major was.

YAY! HERE WE GO!

I gave him a huge smile and announced, "Communication with a concentration in Public Relations."

"Oh," Trev said. "So you're majoring in unemployment?" A light laugh followed.

I froze. Shocked, confused, sad, uncomfortable. He was serious—and clearly didn't pick up on the high I was on, or maybe he did, but was unphased if he destroyed it.

Really thinking about what Trev said, I still felt confident about my decision. *I felt like me—finally.* I was okay with "majoring in unemployment" rather than taking additional math classes so I could switch to the College of Business or continue to float in the College of Arts and Sciences as a sophomore with no major attached to my name.

I don't remember how I responded to Trev because the pride of standing up for myself mixed with the fear of me owning who I am caused me to black out while talking.

Imagine if I let this one person's comment make me overthink the first decision I made in college that helped me finally feel like I fit in?

During my junior year, I continued to do all the fun, nerdy things I loved. Planner obsessed—scheduling and writing *every* little thing down in its spot, writing when I would meet friends for lunch or dinner weeks in advance. And I started a blog, danielleweekly.com, committing to one blog post a week. *Everyone else* I knew at the time with a blog considered themselves a blogger. They wanted to monetize their work and *be known as an influencer* (before we were even labeling them as influencers).

I craved an outlet to talk about experiences with little feedback, without being too public for people around me to actively judge. I can picture myself sitting at my desk like it was yesterday—curled up in my chair with a blanket, knees against the desk, typing away on my laptop, and sipping on a hot cup of tea. However, once the blog existed, and I talked about it with people close to me, I opened myself up to unsolicited feedback.

We're told how we're supposed to do things, or how certain life events are supposed to play out, but it never seems to happen that way. We live in this constant cycle of feeling like we are not enough—*not doing enough, not getting enough, not being enough.* This is exactly where the paralysis or hesitation of posting to social media kicks in.

"I saw your blog post," Noah's mom, Tia (my college boyfriend's mom), told me. "You said you have a lot to say, so you wanted to write more. What do you have to say? You are so quiet," she said, laughing.

Cue the eye roll while also holding back tears.

Comments like this didn't stop me. I continued to share my feelings and perspectives on life. Sharing in this way is so much more than the act of *posting* or *consuming* social media. It's about finding out who you are as a person, what your brand represents, and what you stand for in this world. For me, blogging was a form of therapy. This is the power of sharing experiences; You get to decide how you want to share and consume.

During college, I spent three *full years* with extreme expectations for myself, over-planning and over-delivering.

"Danielle, can you do this and this and this and this?"

For three years, I consistently said yes. While I don't regret a single yes, I was tired of agreeing solely because I didn't want to let people down or miss an opportunity that could have completely changed my life. Honestly, I was just exhausted.

So, rather than going on a fun mini shopping spree or something for a weekend to pat myself on the back for my *hard work,* I treated myself to a whole year of strictly fun.

During my senior year, ya girl quit *everything.* And by *fun* during that time, I mean drinking alcohol daily, eating anything in sight, hanging with friends 24/7, and gaining a Senior 15 (which also meant not being able to fit in any of my jeans and committing to *only* yoga pants).

Employers didn't necessarily like that part of my college experience, so I usually left that out during interviews.

I did *some* work, like studying for exams while at the bar, and half-ass applying for jobs, but I never worried about finding a job *too much.* Trusting I had enough "on my resume" to show what kind of kick-ass, full-time employee I would be one day, I wanted a full year to fully love and embrace being a free version of myself.

I had friends in all different *cliques*. Having a friend for all scenarios was honestly one of my favorite parts of college: going out, grabbing coffee, being lazy, drinking, watching movies, eating snacks, going to the gym, getting late-night milkshakes. By this point, college was about life outside of classes.

But, then you leave college and *BOOM*, you "enter the real world." Apparently you weren't real before you had a degree, as society likes to try to tell us. And cue your first major identity crisis. Your brain is like "school school school school school, now what?" Now your decisions are completely your own.

Who will you become when someone isn't telling you exactly who to be?

The guardrails are gone. No guidelines, no right answers.

Only your intuition.

2. What's Going On?

Writing this book has provided me with so much closure on the latest chapter of my life and has given me so much peace about my past. Mainly writing, rereading and editing has taught me my philosophy of life—I naively existed, thinking *everyone* lives and leads life similarly to my perspective until I realized they weren't. The way I've lived my life has seemed *so simple*—where anyone can follow their intuition and enjoy the outcome, yet no one seems to say this is a valid option to choose to live.

Life will take you all over the place, leading you to do things you never thought you'd do. You will say yes to things you may have never thought would come into your existence and experience things you never imagined, good and bad.

This became abundantly clear to me while laying in bed watching Netflix when I *should have been applying for jobs after graduating college*. My career counselor advised me against grad school since I had already done *enough* internships. Realizing I used to have my schedule locked from 7am to 12pm daily, including weekends, for three years straight, to match the year I had, I treated myself to a full summer off, which was going great until my mom burst into my room.

"Danielle, you're welcome for oversharing about your life on Facebook," my mom said to me in the middle of my *"job search."* All throughout college, my mom regularly shared my posts and pictures, celebrating me on her Facebook page. I'm thankful she wanted to do that, never allowing in the fear of others thinking she was bragging. She just happily shared experiences.

My mom received a Facebook message from a friend, Brit, whose son was on the same lacrosse team as my brother. Brit was the Vice President of Communications at the Alzheimer's Association Connecticut Chapter. She had fought to establish a position under her, and her boss finally approved it.

"I'm not sure if Danielle found a job yet," Brit said, "But if not, I'd love for her to work with me. I've seen your posts about her college experience throughout the last four years. She would be a great fit!"

HELL YEAH.

The following week, I went in and met with Brit. I learned the job had various communications and marketing responsibilities: social media, website content, television and radio ads, billboard creation and placement, flyers, posters, event planning and more. The job felt perfect for me; it also meant I didn't have to pick a track with my communication degree like *everyone* had been telling me. *I could do it all.*

Except for two men, the nonprofit had an all-women staff. So naturally, the office had a strong feeling of community.

I landed my first job opportunity because my mom was "oversharing" on Facebook. How is this happening? LOL.

I started the job during the last week of July 2017. I felt comfortable working for Brit. I had a lot of responsibilities, but I knew I had a great mentor to turn to if I ever got stuck.

Three months later, Brit announced she was leaving for another job.

Fuck, I thought. *This is the person who's supposed to teach me all the things I need to be successful in the industry. Now what?*

At her new job, however, Brit's boss asked her to build her own marketing team—and she invited me to go with her. While touring the office, I had this voice in my head; *if I want to hang on to any form of mentorship, I have to follow her. If I didn't, who else was going to teach me?*

Just then, a strange thought popped into my head and it wouldn't leave me alone. *Maybe I don't need anyone to teach me. What if I just trusted myself?*

I felt confident I knew enough and could pick up new skills and processes.

I decided to stay at the Alzheimer's Association.

Alone.

Twenty-two years old.

No boss.

No idea who was going to be my next mentor.

On my first day unsupervised, the nonprofit's CEO, Katie, pulled me into her office.

"Within the few months you've been here, you've proven you know what you're doing. Danielle, we trust you. We won't be hiring another communications person," Katie continued. "You'll slowly transition into the role."

I was so surprised. I couldn't believe what she said. Even though I trusted Katie and loved how she believed in me, my limiting beliefs were taking over my brain. After all, I was *just out of college.* Trusting myself was hard. I wondered; *how could I possibly be qualified for a position where someone with exponentially more experience had been doing?*

Transitioning from Communications and Public Policy Coordinator into Communications Manager meant handling a budget of nearly $100,000, writing on-stage program scripts for seven fundraising walks across the state of Connecticut, and diving headfirst into all things public relations. These responsibilities were in addition to my other duties.

Each day was a new adventure, and I did *everything* possible to avoid overthinking or second guessing myself. There were plenty of opportunities for me to give up or tell Katie to hire someone else.

But I never did.

I accepted this as my new reality, and I *chose to* focus on trusting myself and believing I was the best person for the role. My CEO trusted me, Brit trusted me enough to want me on her new team, and also trusted my decision to stay. Now, it was time for me to trust I was where I was supposed to be.

Oh, yeah. Don't worry. I eventually I had a boss assigned to me, LOL.

Despite having a PR dream job, it had been a year and a half of living *at home* after college and I was one more eye-roll scenario away from deciding I needed my own place. I used to tell anyone who would listen that I wouldn't be moving out of my parents' house until I paid off alllllll my student loans. The more I told people, the more I tried to convince myself I *should*, even though that's not what I wanted to do.

Overthinking things or doing endless research is never really a part of my decision-making process with anything. I just *do*. It's not easy for me to rely on someone else's opinion like a family member, friend, or a random person on the internet to figure out what is best for me.

If I wanted to remain in a positive headspace for myself, I knew I had to trust my intuition. Once the idea of moving out was in my head, I had to move out *immediately*—the thought wouldn't go away. When something like that happens, my instincts and intuition show up, and I don't let them leave.

I knew I had to commit myself to this decision and keep my forward momentum. I started looking for apartments online immediately, and the next day, I was on the phone with someone. The day after, I toured and signed the lease. I trusted my process, and within a few weeks, I moved into a one-bedroom apartment across town. My parents didn't believe I was seriously moving until I was gone.

Instead of stressing out, I embraced not having a *perfect* apartment, like what people seem to show online. What I couldn't have predicted at the time was the positive impact my network would have on the move.

In case you haven't picked up on this fully by now, *weird and unexpected* things can happen when you share on social media. In this case, Facebook: "I'm moving into my own apartment and if anyone would love to donate some things around their house they never use anymore, I'd be so appreciative!"

I literally went "shopping" for free at a neighbor's house. I've never met her before, but my mom and I drove past her house, and Claire had a ton of furniture on the side of the road, so we stopped.

"I'm getting married and moving in with my husband," she told us. "Go ahead and walk through the house. Take whatever you want for free! We already have what we need for our move."

Friends and family donated almost all my new belongings—silverware, pots and pans, a bed, furniture.

The *only* thing I bought personally was a couch (which ended up being a little over $1,000 after taxes, warranty, delivery and installation —my largest purchase to date at the time) and a blender.

I loved the opportunity to move out, but what I loved even more was the fact that I could swallow my pride, ask my network for help, and not be so stressed about money in the process.

My apartment was in no way luxurious, but I loved it. It was directly above a bar, playing live music more often than I'd like. When there was no live music, the DJ was so loud my wine glasses would clink together. Needless to say, most nights I had a hard time falling asleep. The environment, though, was better for me than staying at my parent's house. The messy, non-aesthetic, makeshift apartment was more than I could have asked for.

I trusted my intuition—I trusted what I was doing and recognized my actions were exactly what I needed to do for myself in the moment. The goal of the shift was to make myself feel like a better version of myself, not to get validation from what others thought this part of my journey *should* look like.

I was happy with where I was in life, but I noticed a hunger for more growth. I wanted to be around people who had the same feelings and approach to life I did. I was looking for my next move, one where I could feel more alive. But I did not know what that meant. All I knew was I wanted to be *more me, more often.*

Allowing this desire to drive my decisions, I found myself attending the Tony Robbins Unleash the Power Within (UPW) Conference in New Jersey in the fall of 2018. A jam-packed, five-day event with 20,000+ attendees, all with the same goal in mind: to learn more about who we were as individuals. I wanted to surround myself with different people and different ways of thinking and learning, the ones I'd dream about growing up. I felt instantly connected. Those in attendance were open to learning about other peoples' vulnerabilities, challenges and successes, while also being open to sharing their own.

Shortly before the conference, I connected with a woman in a Facebook group from California named Addison, who was a few years older than me and also attending the conference. We shared a hotel room together for four nights with the intention of saving money. This was the first time I made a decision like this before—*share a room with a complete stranger, WHAT?* Despite being strangers, it wasn't awkward. Both of us embraced this high-on-life mindset, excited about the matched energy. The level of excitement Addison had about her life was a refreshing feeling to receive from another woman.

The point of the conference was to disconnect from my current reality so I could focus on my future reality.

Two days into the conference, my phone rang for the first time. I didn't recognize the phone number but something inside me was telling me, *pick up the call!!!!!*

It was the General Manager (GM) from the Hartford Yard Goats, a Minor League Baseball (MiLB) team in Connecticut. Cameron and I had met briefly months ago at the ballpark for an Alzheimer's Awareness Night with the Alzheimer's Association.

"Danielle, I've been following you on your personal social media and the accounts for your current job," Cameron explained. "A position has opened up and I think you'd be a great fit. I'd love to have you come in and talk more about the opportunity."

What the fuck.

"Are you sure you have the right Danielle?" I asked. "This is Danielle Chylinski."

I could feel his smile through the phone. He hadn't called the wrong Danielle, but damn, was I caught off guard. *I used my personal social media to share my day-to-day life. I hadn't consciously been using it as personal marketing. This is awkward,* I thought to myself.

I promised Cameron I would think about the position and schedule a time to talk to him in person.

I spent the next couple days of the conference allowing the offer to sink in. I was fully being *me*, and the conference reinforced that I wanted to be nothing less than that feeling. Ever.

After I got home, I revisited the idea of quitting my current job to become the Promotions and Marketing Manager for the Hartford Yard Goats.

Hmmm. I barely play or watch sports. Aside from being there at the event for my job, the only other times I attend games is on social occasions, usually semi-drunk—and I never pay attention to what is happening on the field. Yet, here I am, entertaining the possibility of a marketing role where I would dedicate my face to their social media pages with 30,000+ followers. I'm being trusted with potentially running and overseeing all on-field promotions. How? The job opportunity doesn't seem real. If I say yes, I'd risk being accused of not being qualified, since I don't even like sports. If I say no, I'd get told I had turned down the Hartford Yard Goats, the opportunity of a lifetime.

As I was considering the offer, I met with Cameron and spoke with him over the phone. I bombarded him with a bunch of questions:

"Why would I quit my 9 to 5 job and make my life crazy?"

"Why would I leave my female-dominated nonprofit to go work with mostly men?"

"Why would I ever consider taking a pay cut?"

"Why would I go work in an industry I know nothing about?"

"Are you sure you *actually* want me to work for and with you?"

I felt bad because as soon as Cameron answered one question, I had two more for him.

At *only* twenty-three, I had a *perfect* work-life balance. I woke up, went to work, ate a healthy lunch, loved my coworkers, rocked a PR person's dream job, made solid money, worked out consistently, ate a healthy dinner, hung out, slept, and repeated it all the next day.

I had mastered my original challenge: *graduate college, land a job, and get my shit together.*

But, I was also aware I hit a ceiling. I was told, without a Master's degree, I couldn't earn more and could never hold the title of Director with my current employer.

So, if I could no longer grow with the Alzheimer's Association after *only* a year and a half in, then what was I doing? Sure, I was considering taking a pay cut which many would think doesn't make sense, but I was literally at a job with employees praising me for helping others convert their Word Doc into a PDF.

I received many words of affirmation I didn't expect, but was that enough?

After helping my coworker, Zoey, edit a photo directly in her iPhone app, she told me how incredible I was.

You think?

Drew, from Accounting, complained about how he couldn't figure out how to create a calendar invite, so I walked over to his desk and helped.

"How did you do that?" Drew asked, baffled.

To me, these were such small, basic tasks. I thought *everyone* knew how to do them. Coming out of college, I thought I'd be the one learning, not teaching. I was wrong. I needed to stop assuming people knew the things I knew.

How am I naturally helping people? I'm seriously helping? I wondered, also baffled.

The more I recognized my accomplishments, the more I was aware of the lack of new learning.

I encourage you to recognize the moments when people say, "You've made our lives so much easier!" It's easy to miss these moments and not realize the direct impact you've had—but at the same time, notice how you feel about yourself all around in the moment.

I felt stagnant and my gut told me if I continued too much longer down the path I was going, the lack of challenge and growth would make me feel miserable and complacent.

I had plenty of self-doubt. *Danielle, what are you doing? IDK. Are you sure you can do this? IDK. Did you even make a pros and cons list? LOL I've never made one in my life. What do you know about the company or the sport?*

The truth was, I didn't know much about the company, sport, or industry. And by *not much*, I mean *actually nothing*. But the reassurance of knowing my boss knew me based on my consistent social media presence, which authentically aligned with who I was (posting whatever, whenever, wherever, however) weighed heavier in my decision than any other research or experiences ever could. If Cameron knew exactly what to expect from me, who he was going to deal with as a person and professional, and was excited about it, how could I pass up the opportunity?

I had a chance to completely flip my world. So, I took the job. I gave my notice in November, left the Alzheimer's Association in December, and started my new job with the Hartford Yard Goats in January of 2019.

After a full year of working with the Yard Goats, I absolutely loved my new job, *and* I still felt like there was more out there for me to experience.

This brings us to January 2020. After so many little, scribbled notes in my journal, speaking the idea into existence, talking to my family, and making all the excuses of how I didn't know next steps or what to call it, I did it. High School Danielle, the girl who has never even heard of starting a business, was now the proud founder of Chylinski Media, LLC!

Prior to making it legally official, I was already helping people with their social media accounts, content, and marketing. I would do work for free all the time and wasn't fully aware yet of the impact my skills had on people and their companies. Solidifying a real company was the *more* I was looking for.

In my business, I wanted to create a platform where I could share my knowledge, skills, and experiences, and invite people from anywhere and everywhere to reach out for help.

I was living a true dream—working in an industry I never thought of working in, and now starting a business, doing the thing I loved.

However, in March 2020, COVID-19 reached Connecticut, and I began working from home. Then at the end of June, I, along with 20+ other Hartford Yard Goats employees, were furloughed. Thousands of other, full-time, part-time and seasonal, employees went through similar experiences with varying levels of impact on their lives across the country. Cut off. No warning. Zero.

The awkward, "You recruited me, and now I'm on *pause*, what do I do" hit hard for me. Being furloughed is like having the guy you've been seeing suddenly ghost you and now you're just waiting for a text back. Will I get a message tomorrow, three months, six? What if a better, more-well rounded guy comes your way? Do you text back? Do you say you're not interested? Do you tell them you're kinda seeing someone else?

Working for a baseball team 24/7 versus working for myself 24/7 taught me to be aware of how I feel about myself in all situations. Once COVID-19 hit hard, I had the, *Oh shit, I built this company. Now I actually have to do things with it,* thoughts. You know, like make social pages for Chylinski Media, a website, create a logo, decide on brand colors, announce the company exists—*all the things.*

While announcing my company to the world created a lot of anxiety, I loved this "little company" because, as a country, we were experiencing a time where small businesses needed assistance the most, and I could be there.

I wanted to create business partnerships that turned into friendships. All my clients have been referrals, willing to show vulnerability, having open and honest conversations about how I can help take some of the weight off their shoulders. I value people who respect the things I know, and want to learn more, because there was a time where I didn't realize what I knew to be *obvious* to me, would be life changing to others.

Fear is powerful; so powerful that it can keep us stuck because we're afraid of what the results of our actions will be. However, the greater fear does more damage when you're completely clueless about where the first step begins.

I was fearful that if I didn't make the move, I wouldn't feel *myself*. This fear of not experiencing life as *me* has consistently been the motivational factor to push through the uncertainty of the unknown.

There's no easier way than to ask yourself, "What the fuck is going on?" and then step forward into your higher self.

Recognizing External Influence

When you're feeling uncomfortable and the negative self-talk creeps in, it's easier to get in your own way than out. You may talk yourself into what you think something will be prior to allowing the experience to happen, then make a judgment. Sometimes life seems *so hard*, when in reality, it has a lot to do with unlearning what you thought was *normal*.

3. #DontWasteMyTime

Chicken nuggets. When you hear those two words, you feel something. The feeling is different for every person.

I used to go to the drive-thru, not because I was hungry, but because I needed something to make me feel better.

I think back to walking into a CrossFit class and complaining, "Yeah, I literally just ate a 10-piece nugget from Burger King on the way here. This will be fun." I can envision myself laughing, trying to finish my sentence. These were my choices, yet I wasn't happy with them. Did I say those self-deprecating thoughts out loud in hope others would understand my poor performance if I didn't get as many rounds as I *should* have, or push myself hard enough to get a better time?

I didn't realize the role chicken nuggets were playing in my life until I saw my credit card bill. *Yeah...* Sure, I tried to reassure myself I was being *smart* by buying nuggets because they were *only* $1.49 for a 10-piece, but I knew I needed to make changes. I used chicken nuggets to fill a void, to keep my mind off tough questions and decisions.

I made a commitment to myself in January 2018—*I will not eat chicken nuggets for the entire year.*

To help hold myself accountable, the hashtag #DontWasteMyTime lived rent free in my head. I was straight up wasting my own time by binge eating nuggets before and after a workout—a complete wash AND paying a ton of money to do so. Feeling the need to do something bold to hold my awareness on how I was spending my money, time, and energy, I knew I was up for a major challenge. I *desperately* wanted to hold myself accountable to inspire change within my decision-making.

So, *naturally*, #DontWasteMyTime—The mentality of not wasting time by remaining intentional about the respect you deserve from yourself and others—became ingrained in my daily life.

The first time I shared the hashtag was in an Instagram caption: "Let's all collectively agree none of us have our shit together and let's stop putting all this pressure on ourselves because it's exhausting and I'm fucking over it. #DontWasteMyTime."

We love a strong statement.

My Instagram posts never receive a ton of comments. With this post, though, the message resonated strong enough for several people to leave inspired comments, confirming the power I believed the hashtag to have.

As I continued to use the hashtag on social media, it was comforting to see others do the same. I even started using the hashtag during in-person conversations—like at work. I remember walking into a colleague's office at the Alzheimer's Association and telling her about an email I received.

Through her laughter, she said, "Sounds like #DontWasteMyTime to me."

The hashtag didn't become *just another hashtag* that got lost at the bottom of an Instagram post caption; it became a way of evaluating and measuring respect. Until I made it such a *thing*, I hadn't realized I needed to learn to respect myself, my headspace, my time, and other people's time way more than I was used to.

We don't *always* realize, let alone understand, when we are disrespecting another person's time; it seems so simple, but damn, if you think about it, respecting people's time doesn't happen often.

We're taught to sacrifice ourselves for the greater good. Addressing someone's actions makes you seem negative, *they say*. If you asked someone to not waste your time, how do you envision their response?

#DontWasteMyTime can freak people out, be a turnoff, make them defensive, and put a bad taste in their mouth. But why?

Would you feel threatened? Disrespected? Do you feel you don't deserve to have someone be *that* direct and honest with you?

Life isn't about *having* time. It's about *making* time.

Think about an important goal you achieved—a job you went after, a skill you learned, a hobby you wanted to start, a work project you wanted to kick ass at.

You *made* time.

You created space to reach your goal. *You* got what you wanted because you surrounded yourself with people and situations that allowed you to get there. *You* didn't get your college degree by hanging out with anti-college kids. *You* didn't go to the gym regularly by hanging out with friends who made fun of you for wanting to better your health. *You* didn't change career paths by staying friends with people who thought you had to have a job that aligned with your college major. *You* didn't buy a house with your boyfriend by *only* valuing the opinions of your single girl squad. *You* made the time to align your goal with how you wanted to spend your time.

"I know you're so busy, I didn't wanna bother you, but..."

"I'll just take a minute of your time because I know you're busy..."

Say what you need to say without recognizing how valuable someone's time is. You'll show you *actually* respect their time more by taking up less time.

We do not chase.

If you love yourself, you will recognize you *only* want to work and be around people who love you and respect you in return. Anyone worth your time will not make you chase them. If they wanted to follow up, they would.

Even though it's not *always* easy, you'll find yourself in situations where you need to say *yes* to things that make you feel uncomfortable but serve a purpose and say *no* to things that don't fuel your soul. The #DontWasteMyTime mentality applies to both.

While working at the Alzheimer's Association, I had my first radio interview. The interview was pre-recorded. I was going to be in Florida on vacation with two of my college roommates, Nikole and Emilie, when it aired.

A week prior to my interview airing, I locked myself in my boss' office with my notes scattered all over the table, terrified and trying to figure out how I was going to remember facts and figures.

How am I possibly going to know how to answer all the questions that come my way?

I knew little about radio, and I didn't feel I mastered all there is to know about Alzheimer's disease, so it was an adrenaline rush lead-up.

A lot of learning and focus went into this moment. This interview was my time to prove publicly, on behalf of the Association, that I knew what I was talking about as the Communications Manager.

My second day in Florida, Nikole was sleeping in the living room while I shared Emilie's bed with her.

Suddenly, Nikole barged into the room and yelled loud enough to wake me up, "Danielle, your mom heard on the radio you'll be *LIVE* in ten minutes. She tried calling you, but you didn't answer. She's afraid you're about to miss it!"

Ah fuck.

My mom thought I had forgotten about the interview and I was going to sleep through it. She didn't know the interview was pre-recorded, and I hadn't known what time the segment was going to air. It was a blessing my mom called because, if she hadn't, I wouldn't have heard my first radio interview.

I got out of bed quick, met Nikole in the living room, and laid on the ground listening to the 10-minute interview like two little girls—on our stomachs, feet in the air, smiles so huge our cheeks hurt.

Once it was over, we jumped on the couch and danced around the room in celebration.

Emilie stood in the doorway staring. "Why are you awake *so* early and being *so* loud?"

"I was on the radio for the first time a second ago! Didn't you hear Nikole wake me up? We're literally jumping for joy!" I cheered, continuing to jump on Emilie's couch.

"Okay, well, you're so loud. Can you not?" Emilie said, closing the door to crawl back into bed.

There was no way I was going to let anybody kill my vibe, not after how proud I was of my interview. So, Nikole and I kept smiling, bouncing and dancing away.

This interview was a pivotal event in my life—the beginning of my media career and one of my best friends from college *decided to* sleep through it, despite how much Nikole and I were celebrating. The happiness was extremely apparent, yet Emilie couldn't feel the happiness *for us*, so living the happiness *with us* wasn't an option.

I kept repeating the scenario in my head. *My friend chose to be annoyed and go back to bed instead of enjoying a milestone with me. Why was I choosing to be friends with her?*

Long story short, I said bye-bye-bye to my friendship with Emilie when my plane landed back at home a few days later.

This is a part of post-college 101, where you learn some people continue with you on your journey while others no longer align. Pay attention and stay aware of how you feel when you're in certain situations or around certain people and how they react when you feel a certain way, especially when you're feeling happy or celebrating.

There were many times where I felt liberated, betrayed, so excited I brought myself to tears, or extremely sad where I felt unbearably numb. I'd think to myself, *Who was I around in those moments?*

You're allowed to say no to continuing a friendship with someone who makes you doubt yourself and question your self-worth. You already know who you are inside; Don't look to other people to tell you. Feel free to *politely* put them in the trash.

In college, I would have apologized to Emilie for being too loud. I might have even missed listening to the interview in fear of waking her up.

But in this situation, I shifted my thinking.

I was finally happy with who I was, the work I put in and what I was doing professionally. No one was going to take *me* away from me. My thinking shifted from blaming others for my poor experiences to allowing my disappointments to come from within. I no longer let external factors take control of me; I take full ownership of my narrative.

I started digging deeper within myself to uncover the reasoning for the situations I put myself in, then I *let that shit go*.

We carry a lot on our shoulders, and it's extremely heavy.

Have you ever considered that sometimes the weight isn't yours to carry?

Progress comes from breaking patterns. Implementing habits. Pushing through on the hard days. Finding others who can hold you accountable and celebrate your wins, big and small.

Evaluate the relationships in your life and reflect on how they make you feel. You might not realize how heavy some of your relationships are until they are no longer weighing on you.

I understand the "but they've been my best friend for years" is a fun narrative to hold. However, it doesn't matter how long you've known someone.

Choose people who help you reach a state that keeps you at your best. Make adjustments as needed, guilt free.

Doubt and comparison show up *everywhere*: jobs, employers, customers, clients, family and friends. Recognizing relationships change is important.

The thoughts run through your head; *Can I trust them? How much is too much? Am I oversharing?*

People are in different parts of their life and doing different things. So then you think; *Will they be excited for me? Will they understand my point of view? Will they get annoyed with me? Will they get jealous and weird?*

Finding balance in life becomes much easier once you are aware and take control of *your* reality.

4. Triggered AF

"I want to wake up earlier *every* day."

These words came out of my mouth at the UPW Conference and 18-year-old Clay heard me. He asked me why, so I told him.

"I want to feel like I have control of my mornings and not feel rushed. I want to stop putting mascara on while I'm driving to work and walking into the office with wet hair."

"Okay, let's do this," Clay said. Clay offered to call me *every* morning to wake me up and stay on the line until I was fully awake, out of bed, and ready to start my day.

I stood there, speechless, looking at him like, *are you fucking nuts*, but he was so serious without hesitation.

He followed through.

Every day, for a month, he called me at six o'clock in the morning.

After a month, I woke up on my own, no problem.

Later, I learned he was living on the West Coast, waking up *three hours earlier*, complaint free, while I complained about not being able to wake up at six o'clock.

What the actual fuck; I know.

Clay was committed to helping me get rid of my limiting belief, and he became a friend to do it.

My belief that I couldn't change my routine and wake up early was a *limiting belief*—something you hold to be true but is far from reality and negatively affects your growth.

A belief is something accepted, *considered to be true*, or held as an opinion.

Sounds simple as hell, but how often are we questioned by others about what our beliefs are?

Whether you're scrolling through social media, attending a conference, listening to a podcast, deep in conversation, or consuming content some other way, many external factors contribute to what we consider concrete.

Even though we all have beliefs, they aren't *always* true. And to make matters more complicated, we are not *always* aware of them, either.

I constantly let my friends down.

I can't possibly be qualified for this job.

There's no way I can start my own business.

We can be unaware of the narratives we tell ourselves, yet they're driving factors of how we choose to live our lives. It's hard when you realize something you've believed to be true for years isn't. We can blame our past, do nothing, and stay stuck, or we can take control of our lives and understand what's most important to us.

Learning how to sit in silence with our thoughts and feelings gives us an opportunity to ask ourselves, *Are my beliefs actually mine? What do I believe and live by as rules that might instead be an opinion or thought that isn't helping me achieve my goals?*

When I founded Chylinski Media, I did it for myself, by myself, with no expectation anyone would support, show support, or know how to support me. In operating from this space of having no expectations, each comment and message brought me joy.

Tackle your limiting beliefs for yourself, not for someone else. Your reactions correlate to your beliefs.

I firmly believed Moe's had the best queso, without question. *Every* type of queso I'd try, I would compare and decide, "Well, I still like Moe's better." Suddenly, Chipotle launched their queso—a new competitor entered the market.

Somebody I knew and trusted told me, "OMG, Chipotle's queso is gross. Don't bother spending your money or stomach on it."

So, I believed her. I believed her so much that I refused to buy Chipotle chips and queso... for years.

I'd think; *Moe's is only a couple minutes down the road from Chipotle, so I'll get a bowl at Chipotle then chips with queso from Moe's.*

I spent years justifying to myself why I wouldn't give the Chipotle queso a try.

The same thing can apply to people.

We build these perceptions of people before meeting them based on the opinions of others. Even when they're opinions from people we value and respect, they are still beliefs we are creating without fully knowing the situation. It's a limit we impose on ourselves. We limit ourselves from continuing or expanding experiences that might be awesome.

You're *only* holding yourself back and closing yourself off from opportunities.

The first step in dealing with your limiting beliefs is to become aware of them.

The second step is to identify which beliefs are reality versus adopted beliefs (unintentionally believed to be *a fact)*, using the knowledge of your limiting beliefs to help you get there.

Once you've compared your *adopted* beliefs with your *limiting* beliefs, you'll recognize change needs to happen to begin operating under the narrative of your *true* beliefs.

The hardest part? Leaning in and committing to change.

Sometimes you'll find yourself in a situation where you don't have the option to lean on someone else or ask for support. It's you, and you alone, in that moment.

During my first week working for the Hartford Yard Goats, I was deep into learning a new language (sports, specifically baseball), the workflow, pace, the different personalities of my colleagues and the new atmosphere as a whole.

When I accepted the job, I knew nothing about Minor League Baseball. *Could the Yard Goats play the Yankees? Could a Yard Goats player ever be a Yankees player? I need answers.*

Part of the job included making graphics of the starting lineup for the home team to post on social media every game—*home* (70 games) and *away* (70 games). 70+70=140 games.

It was quite the process, but long story short, I had to wait for the lineup to be sent to me by the radio broadcaster.

If you've ever seen a lineup, it's not always as clear as you would hope. There are numbers everywhere. Numbers that mean *positions*. Numbers that I had no idea what they meant.

My coworker who sat next to me in the office wrote on a sticky note which position corresponded with which number; I taped it right next to my mouse pad on my laptop. I read the note every single game—all 140 games during the season.

To this day, though, I still don't have the numbers and positions memorized, whoops.

I valued my coworker so much since he chose to respect that I didn't know shit, he gave me a cheat sheet to make my life easier, as opposed to disrespecting or making fun of me for not knowing as much as others.

I didn't even know what homestand meant (the number of games in a row the team plays). *But I also knew nothing about Alzheimer's until I began working for the nonprofit. They still trusted me with their brand voices and social media accounts,* I'd constantly think to myself.

I felt overwhelmed as I learned to navigate all the new unknowns of my job (which was *everything*).

Then, during my first month, my boss asked me to work at a Goat Yoga event (as in doing yoga with actual baby goats) taking place at the ballpark. My *only* task was to take pictures for social media.

"Definitely," I told my boss. "I'm in. Sounds super fun."

Halfway through the event, I got a call from the president.

"A reporter from NBC Connecticut is at the ballpark. They want someone to interview on behalf of the organization."

3 seconds of silence filled the call on both ends.

"You're the *only* person in the building right now qualified to do the interview."

Qualified? I thought to myself. *What happened to my only task being to take pictures?*

I came from a PR background where interviews with no preparation were never a good idea, especially as a woman. You'd create your talking points document and go over them hundreds of times before you aired. All eyes were on you because *there's a woman and not a man speaking on behalf of sports on TV?* Those watching are listening extra closely, staring, subconsciously waiting for you to mess up.

My PR classes taught me I needed to make sure I am *always* in a position to best represent the company, and that meant preparing before speaking to the media live.

I'm not capable, I thought to myself. *How the fuck am I supposed to talk about why people should come to the ballpark when I don't even know why I'm at the ballpark?*

I had no legitimate reason to say no and honestly, in that moment, what did I have to lose

"On it," I replied. "I got it covered."

I was transparent with the woman reporter.

"This is my first month in this position, but I'll do the best I can."

This wasn't ideal for my first media appearance at my new job, but the interview ended up being great. I could have easily believed I couldn't do it, panicked, and said no. Instead, I told myself I *was* capable. The president had told me I was qualified—so *I had to* believe I was qualified.

Change can be awkward when what you need to change seems overwhelming—how you think, what triggers you, and how you react to something based on what you believe to be a fact.

I treated the job like I would treat any other situation and didn't think less of myself because I was a woman. Hearing limiting beliefs from other women around me in the workplace though, had made me second guess my beliefs.

Should I be thinking, speaking and acting how the other women are?

I watched some surrounding women in the sports industry think less of themselves, shrink themselves down, and change how they acted and responded in certain situations. They had to work twice as hard to convince themselves they belonged there. This type of limiting belief is heart-breaking, and women *everywhere* face it.

Countless times in conversation, my female colleagues would comment things like:

"I mean, after all, it is a male dominated industry for a reason."

"They would have listened to my idea if I had a dick."

"If I suggested that idea, no one would have liked it. But since he did, of course, *everyone's* clapping."

"I'm *only* in the meeting because they need a note-taker, not because they value my contribution."

Facts? Maybe.

I heard them, but I wasn't really listening.

I'm not trying to be a woman in a male dominated industry; I'm just being Danielle Chylinski—existing as her in the world. Some didn't like that—challenging themselves to wrap their head around my reality—unrelatable and not their reality, while others understood.

Once you're aware of how limiting beliefs are affecting *you, you'll* realize other people are regularly affected by their own limiting beliefs. *Your* awareness will help *you* gain confidence. Get out of *your* own way. *Your* beliefs will trigger *your* reactions, and what *you* choose to focus on has the power to change your day. *You're* going to treat the people in *your* path based on how *you're* feeling.

The outside world doesn't control *your* feelings—*you* do.

Blaming, complaining, or hurting someone else won't help.

When you control your internal world by aligning your beliefs with your true self, you remove the triggers the external world has over you.

You'll *always* experience influence over your feelings, but you will also *always* remain in control.

5. Like Plants Growing Through Concrete

"Will you run for freshman class treasurer? Tess is running for President, I'm running for Secretary, and Vanessa is running for Vice President. We want you to be Treasurer."

The last thing I would want to do is to be responsible for any of the math work associated with being treasurer for the entire freshman class in my high school, I thought to myself.

"Please, we *need* you to."

"Sure," I said. "I'll run."

Inside, I was screaming at myself. *What, Danielle? What! Why would you ever agree to this?*

I *actually* wanted to run, not *run.*

Thoughts spun through my head. *Did everyone else think I was good at math? Did I like that they thought I was? Will someone more qualified than me realize they should have this position, not me?*

The imposter syndrome was *rough* once I won the election unopposed. I was embarrassed knowing that being Class Treasurer screamed *math* and all my report cards screamed *not math.*

Except, none of my classmates saw my report card. All they knew was that I was taking geometry, the highest level freshman math class. The difference between how I saw myself and how *everyone* else saw me represented different realities.

"Can I stay after school today to do my homework?" I'd ask my math teachers (Freshman, Sophomore, Junior & Senior year of high school). I knew I would never do the homework, never mind finish it, if I took it home—delaying the work, getting stuck in my anxiety.

You know that feeling when you are trying to figure out how to complete a task but are too afraid to ask for help?

Prior to asking for a little extra supervision in math class, I'd come to class day after day embarrassed about not having more than half of my homework done. *Please don't call on me,* I'd say over and over in my head, incredibly uncomfortable in my skin when the teacher would go through the assignment.

My freshman year of high school, I failed the last quarter of geometry. *Failed. F.* The letters on my report card from the prior quarters all started with the same first letter of my first name: *D.*

Yet, *every single year*, my classmates re-elected me as Class Treasurer. I was *always* afraid someone would figure out my secret and yell, "Wait, this girl seriously has no idea how to do math?"

But instead of the possibility of being called out pushing me to quit, I owned it. I didn't parade around sharing what I viewed as a weakness, yet I allowed myself to be open with others in the right moments. Doing so took the weight of feeling like a fraud off my shoulders.

This reminds me of a former friend, Ellie. Five years into a committed relationship and newly engaged, Ellie wasn't sure how to be more affectionate with her fiance. I was shocked she felt that way for so long and hadn't talked about it with him. What will happen if Ellie starts a conversation with him about how she feels? What if she doesn't?

Will she settle for zero hugs and cuddles for the rest of her life until she falls out of love and they get divorced because she was too awkward to ask? I didn't have any advice besides *how could you let it get to this point?*

There are *always* going to be things in life that *haunt* you. It's your choice whether you want to learn what lies on the other side of that opportunity. There is also *always* the option to walk away... and never know what life would have looked or felt like, or how it could have shaped your life. The opportunities presented to you are *only* as big as they seem based on your limiting beliefs and false perceptions.

When your mindset shifts from needing constant external validation to having full control of your thoughts and emotions, you'll begin to attract more opportunities. You can raise your consciousness through reflection and intention setting. Sometimes you'll realize what you thought you wanted—in your career, in your relationships, in any and all the choices you make—isn't what you want anymore.

Embrace the change and opportunities. Focus on attracting what you want.

My fear of math carried into deciding my major, yet *somehow* I now own a business in which I encounter math all the time.

Before having a bookkeeper, I double and triple checked numbers daily. (Shocked my first big business expense was a bookkeeper?) I was constantly in self-doubt mode.

Did I charge this right? Did I transfer the correct amount? Does this add up? I sent that to my business checking, not personal checking, right? Oh shit, did I forget to add tax to that?

I was reminded of my math homework in highschool, my terrible grades and my *not-good-enough* GPA.

Sometimes, and *almost always*, you, too, will never know the value of a moment until it becomes just a memory.

This is exactly how I felt about my experience working in Minor League Baseball.

Experiencing what it's like to grow, to *actually feel* a change within myself—mentally, spiritually, physically, emotionally—was new to me. I used to joke about the job being the dream job I never knew I had. But truthfully, it was.

My relationships and skills grew as I found myself constantly breaking old habits and replacing them with new ones. Amidst *always* fighting so many emotions, I'd envisioned the results of my goals for the position and demanded a different version of myself, from myself, in order to reach them.

I didn't know the impact deciding to take this job would have on me until my world came to a halt in 2020. Since I never imagined working in baseball, I appreciated each moment I had at work. While the abrupt furlough was tough, I also felt at peace knowing I gave my all to this job, and I saw this new situation as an opportunity instead of an obstacle.

For me, each day working at the ballpark was a day to celebrate.

As a society, we tend to *only* celebrate the grand milestones: graduations, engagements, baby showers, birthdays. We give little thought to the outcome or future afterwards and celebrate anyway. Why isn't the experience similar for starting things: a store, a podcast, a new job, a clothing line? In these cases, we are unsure of the outcome, so we're scared to share.

As humans, we get scared sharing exciting milestones will look like we're *bragging*, which often leads to minimizing the strong success we are achieving.

You're afraid that by sharing things that make *you* happy, someone will think negatively of you?

Read that again.

If that's the case, do you even want someone like that in your circle? Do you want to validate them? Or even care about their opinion, letting *them* drive your decision making?

I had a client say to me once, "I have had so many breakdowns between this week and last. But I've also had so many breakthroughs." Felt that.

What you celebrate, how you celebrate, and why you celebrate is entirely up to you. Want to go out and get a drink with friends? Want to stay inside and watch movies all day because you did one thing today as opposed to nothing? Want to write in your notebook daily, documenting each emotion you feel?

Literally do whatever the fuck you want. Any choice works as long as you're happy with the outcome.

We often get caught up in external life instead of staying caught up with ourselves.

I'm into genuine authenticity. I've outgrown the expectations I have for some people (compared to the reality of who they are) and relationships I tried to continue that *only* dragged me down.

"Are you guys psyched about life or what?" I asked the group of 100+ student leaders during a speaking engagement at my alma mater. They seemed almost confused and in shock. Their responses were *less than* enthusiastic.

I want a potential client and those I have interactions with to hang up the phone, bounce off the walls hyped up, in love with me and the relationship we're about to form. I want them to love the thought of changing their own life for the better (with my support).

That's the thing about entrepreneurship—building a business is *hard* and extensive, but you get to decide how you want to show up for yourself and others, as well as who you want to be showing up for.

The challenge translates to personal life too.

Within the same week of moving out into my new apartment, I was having car trouble. My car guy, Joe, told me my transmission could *go* any day; it could break tomorrow or could break in two years.

"To be safe, I'd look for a new car, but *no rush*," Joe told me.

To my dad, though, getting a new car was a *rush*. He worried I was going to be stranded, stuck, or in a dangerous spot.

Jokes on me, I was so incapable of making any sort of educated decision for myself, so I was like, "Yeah sure, love this for me. Let's go car shopping for a car I definitely cannot afford."

So, car shopping I went. My mom offered to help me look. Her and I were trying to figure out what made the most sense with my low budget. I attempted to allow my brain to accept I was going from no car payment to a significant one, days after having to now pay monthly rent.

My dream car is one I could show up to places looking professional, clean and organized; I thought to myself.

Literally though, that's what I told my car salesperson, and he was like *???*

I've never actually been one to dream about material things, like a specific brand or model car or what I *wanted to be seen* driving in. My current car was a 2005 blue shiny Subaru Legacy; I loved it. I figured I'd stick with Subarus since that's where my comfort level was—why not?

While we were looking, one car totally fit a vision I didn't know I had: A white 2019 Subaru Legacy with heated seats, heated steering wheel, and a sunroof.

Then, out of nowhere, like literally out of nowhere, this other car showed up: a 2019 Gray Honda Civic. Nothing special. Just your basic car, but $5,000 less than the white Subaru.

Somehow within *minutes*, I was signing to buy this Honda Civic because my parents told me it was the most sensible financially (as in most sense financially for *my finances* because I was paying) all without them knowing how I handle my money, what my salary was, or how much I had in the bank. K.

Yet, here I was, a 23-year-old adult with a full-time job and now my own apartment, letting my non-paying parents tell me what was best for me financially.

"Heated seats, heated steering wheel, and a sunroof? You do not need that. That's a luxury and unrealistic."

Unrealistic to make sure my usually cold body was warm in the winter and my hair would blow in the wind in the summer? Was it unrealistic, though? What about considering luxury made it unrealistic for me? Why didn't I deserve luxury?

I knew to my core I could have strongly benefited from *luxury features*. For whatever reason, I doubted my judgment and trusted my parents' more.

"Sure Danielle, maybe your life would have been better with those few features, but not for $5000. You're being so dramatic."

Was I though? I was speaking into existence what I knew would help my days be better, what would help me be me, and then I blatantly ignored it when I had the chance to choose otherwise. Ugh.

I should have put myself first, committed to what made ME happy, but instead, I let myself believe other people's ideal view of security and practical decisions dictate my life.

Or maybe, like, take a minute Danielle. Why did you need to make a decision right then and there? What would life be like if I didn't?

I like to think I would have felt extremely happy. I would have many hours of my life back, for all those times I couldn't find my new gray car among the other thousands of gray cars in literally almost every parking lot I've ever parked in... but anyway... I let the law of attraction do its thing, and kept in the back of my mind that eventually I wanted a different car that made sense for me, not for anyone else. When I had the chance to change my narrative, I did.

I sold my Honda Civic in August 2020, about 2.5 years after purchasing. My boyfriend had a work car, and was going back and forth on selling his personal car, a Red Jeep Grand Cherokee.

"I'll sell mine instead. I'd love to find *my car* in the parking lot again," I said to him before I could even think about what I just said out loud.

We recently moved in together, and here I was going from *Ms. I don't need no man* to *Yeah I'm going to sell my car and drive yours. Thanks.*

His jeep had all the things that I wanted: heated seats, heated steering wheel, and a sunroof. Felt like true freedom.

Tears were everywhere throughout my car relationship journey.

Even though others try to care about the choices you make, they are consciously only in that state of mind temporarily. Opinions can be thrown out left and right, but with outcomes that impact you directly, you'll be the one getting the hit of the outcome.

Next time, I'm buying the damn thing *I want*—what my intuition is screaming at me to do. And I won't apologize for making a decision that's best for me and how I *want* to live my life.

"Cry if you need to." I tell my clients. "No one *actually* cares if you're crying, though."

Ego aside, cry it out, feel it out, breathe it out, but realize you get to decide what goes on in your life. Learn from the moments. Growth is on the other side of pushing through what seems impossible, whether it seems delusional or not.

As humans, we project our own judgment of ourselves onto others and then make decisions based on what others think.

But what about what *you* think?

6. Not Here to Let Fear Win

When I was in middle school, our class would do an activity called popcorn reading. Popcorn reading is when one person reads a couple paragraphs of a book or short story, then says "popcorn" followed by the name of the person they want to read next. If someone called your name, you'd continue reading where that person left off.

I hated popcorn reading—sitting in my chair and forgetting to breathe, praying to the universe that *every* single person in the class would somehow forget I existed. I didn't want to hear, "Popcorn Danielle."

The fear of having to read out loud, afraid to stumble over my words, look stupid, get laughed at or made fun of was *real*. Quickly in my head, while someone else was reading, I would read the paragraphs ahead and skim through words I may not know, and try to sound them out or understand them before being called on.

Living with that type of fear is hard—and it's hard not to let it win.

However, the not-so-nice middle school boys didn't want to call on the people who seemed confident in reading. They wanted to call on the ones who they knew were panicking. They wanted to call on me.

Sometimes you don't know the fear is there until the fear gets resolved and faced head-on.

Here, the idea of being called on hurt my soul more than *actually* being called on.

When did I grow out of hating popcorn reading? Maybe never, but what changed was my external confidence. How I carried myself switched from *I want to literally jump out the window and run until I reach another universe* to, "Sure dude, call on me. Try to think you're gonna get a good laugh because you won't. Joke's on you for choosing me, looking for entertainment."

Flash forward. I'm working for the Hartford Yard Goats and the president, Jake, told me, "Danielle, we need you to do the seat upgrade during pre-game. All you have to do is find a family, follow a 4-sentence script during a :30 minute on-screen promotion, and award them seats behind home plate."

I thought to myself; *There is no fucking way I'm getting on a microphone in front of thousands of people.*

Pacing back and forth in the promotions room, when I was sure I was going to mess up, a comment Jake had made more than once came back to me.

"What if I mess up?" I would ask.

"So what?" he'd say to me.

So, I gripped the microphone, walked into the stands, and spoke on the big screen as 7000+ people found their seats. That little girl, terrified of popcorn reading, could plant her feet, stand with good posture, be aware of her breathing, and do what she had to do.

How much of the stuff in your head that you're telling yourself is *actually* true?

Your fear of looking stupid is wasting too much time.

Our society is so focused on "what's your major?" when you're in college instead of "what do you need to thrive daily in the workplace?"

This was one of those moments that proved to me I needed supportive coworkers & a healthy work environment where I could be open about my thoughts.

Never have I ever had my heart set on where I wanted to work or what jobs I saw myself doing, or what my dream car, house, location, all the things would be. What mattered—and still matters—the most to me is the environment.

How do I feel when I enter an office? How does my colleagues and clients make me feel? Do I feel empowered? Do I feel supported? Do I feel free to be authentically me? Do I feel comfortable speaking up? Do I feel heard?

Many decisions in my life have been based on instinct, specifically on how I feel about the environment I'm in.

You spend *more time* in the workplace than you do at home. You spend the *most time* talking about the tasks you're doing. You spend the *least time* thinking about the environment you're in and how it affects the work you produce.

Are you a business owner or are you working for someone else? Are you in a typical 9-to-5? Are you starting your workday at six o'clock in the morning and ending at three o'clock in the afternoon? Are you wearing a uniform or ripped jeans and flip-flops? Are you in an office or at home? What environment will allow you to thrive as the best version of you?

What's something you hated or didn't feel strong in, so you chose to avoid it? Or at least for as long as you could.

Some things are unavoidable. Like Research Methods when you're a Communication major. *Cringing at the thought of the class.* Research Methods.

I remember thinking over and over in my head; *There's a 0 percent chance I'm going to pass this class when I saw it on my transcript. I don't do research. It's just not fun to me. The idea of this class is terrifying and frustrating. I usually wait for people to suggest something and then I check it out.*

Why am I so freaked out?

When it came time to pick our topic for our semester long research paper, it seemed each student was talking about choosing topics that seemed to be the *easiest to research*.

I went a different route. I chose a topic I *actually* wanted to research, regardless of the difficulty. In my mind, I needed to love what I was researching in order to face my fear.

There is a significant difference in outcome when you choose something you're interested in versus not.

There were so many classes I never imagined I'd be able to live through.

"Danielle, to complete your minor you need to take this class in the College of Business that focuses on pitching to companies," my career counselor shared with me. "You're going to be on a fake marketing team for a fake company, putting together a fake plan, trying to secure a project. Every 4 weeks, your group, company and project will change. Each project will have a winner. Your team either wins the bid for each project and you get an A, or you lose and get an F."

Excuse me, what?

I learned a lot simply because the subject material was *all* new *to me*. Sentence after sentence that came out of each *business major's* mouth was brand new information *to me*. I was the *only* student in class pursuing a communication major.

In Communication classes, I experienced my classmates wanting to talk, answer questions, and blurt out thoughts.

In the College of Business, it felt like no one wanted to talk, afraid to be wrong—afraid of failure.

During one presentation, a man I recognized walked in. *Crap, I know this guy. Why is he here?*

"Class, please welcome our *fake* client for today," the professor shared out loud.

Oh fuck, I said to myself in my scattered brain. *I'm literally gonna fuck this up so bad.*

I knew him personally from other opportunities I've had on campus outside of academics and knew he thought highly of me. Except what he didn't know was that I'm like the weird ass ugly duckling in the class who *didn't belong* and I was hanging on by a thread to keep up.

Yeah, so the presentation went terribly.

The next day, my professor came up to me and said, "Danielle, the fake client yesterday said he knew you."

I could feel my face getting red. I couldn't find words.

"He could not believe how nervous you were."

"I couldn't believe it either," I said back to my professor.

I mean, *I could believe it, though*.

After reflecting, I really understand why I was so nervous. It's not because I wasn't good enough for the class, or I wasn't good at public speaking. I was nervous because I literally had no clue what the fuck I was talking about. AT ALL. I was already pre-judging my group for being all business students AKA aliens used to different social norms in class who I didn't want to fuck with, but I had to for a grade. I hated the topic and my group didn't feel prepared as we had just spent the last 14+ hours on this entire project, staying up all hours of the night. I had to try my best to impress someone else, get their approval—like my future depended on it, *because it did*.

I wasn't confident about our case to win the bid. I was trying to memorize what I was supposed to say rather than learning and understanding the material, so I panicked. And it showed.

In *the real world*, there is no "trying to memorize" or "learning how to say the right thing." I mean there is, but it's not effective. Memorizing for a moment instead of to retain can *only* get you so far in business and your personal life. The most freeing decision is to speak your truth. It can be uncomfortable, but at least you know what you're saying and believe in it.

Own what you know and what you don't; life straight up becomes easier when you embody this.

Sometimes admitting you're afraid makes it easier on you.

I received an email that seemed so random for someone in their first season of working in sports: "Minor League Baseball would like to formally invite you to the 2019 MiLB Innovators Summit in El Paso Texas and to participate in the Charity Challenge."

This year, there was an emphasis on the Charity Challenge which involved 4 teams of 2 people competing in a few fun races and activities throughout the Summit in front of all the attendees.

I could see it in my head: hundreds of people around me... staring... watching... judging... critiquing. I weighed the pros and cons of saying yes in response to their email, "Danielle, Congratulations! You've been selected to be one of eight Front Office Staff involved in the Charity Challenge at this Summit out of IDK, 1000+?."

I know, sounds terrifying, right?

What was the worst that could happen? What's the best? How will this impact or enhance my experience? If I say yes, I'll get the opportunity to have fun and meet new people, right? If I say no, I'm saying no because I'm afraid; I thought to myself.

Read that again.

The *only* reason I would say no is because I'm afraid.

So I said yes.

Whatttttt.

I know.

After a few days of thinking about it, participating in the challenge was going to be interesting since I *only* ever met like 4 people who were going to be attending the summit LOL.

Well, guess what?

My partner and I ended up winning!

Won. Winners. First place.

The final event of the challenge took place at Southwest University Park, home to the El Paso Chihuahuas. We raced around the field, completing a series of mini challenges with those I had just met in the last 48 hours, in the stands watching, cheering and rooting for us.

After crossing the finish line, they presented us with an oversized check made out to Big Brothers Big Sisters, the charity we were representing.

I thought to myself; *If these people I just met and those I've never met can root for me, I can also cheer myself on.*

A year later, MiLB invited me back to the Innovators Summit, except this time it was completely virtual and I was a speaker. At this point I, like many others in the industry, had been furloughed. MiLB asked me and another furloughed employee from a different MiLB team to co-host a session called "Breaking Back into the Industry."

We designed the presentation for people within the baseball industry, other sport and entertainment professionals, companies, and college students trying to break into sports.

"We'd like to start off by thanking our bosses for furloughing us because if it weren't for them, we most likely wouldn't have been asked to speak at an enormous event like this," I said to the online viewers.

A bold way to start a presentation? Yes.

An honest way to start a presentation? Also yes, *and* I couldn't help myself.

My co-host and I talked about how we got into the sports industry and the difference in our backgrounds. We explained the feeling of being furloughed by our team, quickly and awkwardly "on the outside," sharing our story and feelings to the MiLB world.

MiLB—sounds scary and big, right? Yet, I wasn't scared to present. I didn't overthink the talking points; I didn't overthink who and how many people would be in the room (virtually). It was like talking to hundreds of people who *get it*.

Becoming equal to your fears makes them easier to face. Fear is extremely powerful, but it's not more powerful than you.

Self Awareness

Surround yourself with people who align with what you *actually* want. Be willing to create change when you intuitively feel the need, even though it will cause resistance. Talking about reality negatively will *always* keep you in a miserable state, so what's possible when you change your narrative?

7. Damn Distractions

When I find myself uncomfortable, I look for a distraction. My mom and brother were my distraction when we'd go to the dentist growing up. The waiting room had a ton of LEGOs we'd look forward to playing with while arguing over who gets to go first.

But now, I go to the dentist alone—no LEGOs to look forward to and no brother to fight with. Still, even as an *adult*, I find myself uncomfortable. I'm distraction free from the moment I walk into the building to when there is someone else's hands in my mouth.

I could never understand why, in the midst of being wrist deep in the mouth of their patients, dental hygienists try to have a conversation, constantly asking questions that will naturally go unanswered.

Am I supposed to participate in this conversation, or *am I supposed to attempt an answer to their questions?*

One day, I decided *screw it* and kept talking while my dental hygienist's hands were in my mouth. Rather than staying quiet or not responding to her small talk, I found a way to make the conversation work.

Being present and participating in the conversation was way more valuable than being worried about feeling awkward.

You're allowed to smile, laugh and even talk without having a justified explanation, especially at the dentist. The "You're *always* one decision away from a completely different life" quote is no joke—and you deserve *every* damn second of it. You never know the value each person involved will take away from any connection or interaction.

I've realized running your life and decisions through the filter of other people's perceptions will lead to a mix of contradictory advice.

The following confusion ensures *your* decisions about *your* life are more difficult to make. In response, it's easier to look for distractions than to simply live life on *your* own terms.

Let's say you finally have some extra money to spend, and you decide you want to buy a car. You'll have the people who will say, "Damn bro, you earned this. I'm so happy you saved up and spent money on something you've *always* wanted."

On the flip side, you'll have the, "This kid is so dumb. They just spent *x amount* of dollars on a car. Is that a smart money move?"

BUT, if you didn't get a new car and still drove the beat up 1990-whatever car you had in high school, then you'd get the, "Wow this kid is broke AF," and the "You're saving so much money, I wish I did that" response.

Wild to think about, right? Either way, you lose.

Wrong.

Either way, you WIN. You win *every* situation for yourself and walk away loving your decisions if you truly choose to love and support your own decisions. How fun!? Like seriously, though.

You're in full control, but honoring the emotion is important. It's about being the best you're capable of being and doing so un-apologetically.

We have the power to create moments where we remind ourselves of our worth. Honestly, the "friends" who *hate on you* for continuing to better yourself mentally, emotionally, spiritually and physically, say bye bye bye to them (just dance it out and blame NSYNC).

You deserve better than your inner circle attempting to dim the evolving version of yourself. You know the saying, "they're going to talk anyway, so let's give them something to talk about?" No matter what you do, someone will have something to say, whether it's in support of you or against you.

What society says is *best for you* may not be what's best for you. People project that belief because they may never think it's possible for them... So they put you down, causing you to question yourself.

Internalizing comments from others often becomes a distraction and a roadblock on your journey—if you let it.

The worst is when people are like, "back to reality" after doing something fun...

goes on vacation, comes home

"Back to reality tomorrow (AKA work)"

girls night out on a Saturday, spends the whole Sunday hungover

"Back to reality tomorrow (AKA work)"

Why are we speaking and acting like our "non-reality" is so fun, and our "actual reality" is so bad?

Truth is, they're both your actual reality. You're just having trouble acknowledging you have full control over your mindset. The false societal expectation of your reality shows us we're supposed to have extremely happy and fun days, and then awful, boring, unfulfilling days.

You just don't have to do, feel or believe that. This is where the idea of different realities comes into play.

How would you feel if you were consistently creating and maintaining a life where you can't wait to wake up to?

"My reality" may not be the same as "your reality." It could be, in theory, how we feel about realities... or you could choose it, instead of building and shaping your expectations based on other societal opinions.

Think about it.

You work multiple jobs and it's, "Wow, good for you for working so much and probably saving so much money for your future. I wish I did that," or it's, "You're going to regret working so much when you're young. These are the best years of your life. Live a little."

Life is all about perception, and as we are all different, we all have differing ideas of what our reality *should* look like.

I used to come home from work and the gym, then talk talk talk talk talk to my parents. Next thing you know, it's midnight. Okay, well, not consistently *that late*, but *always* past my bedtime. My mom and dad filled the time and space that was once held by my college roommates.

"How was your day? What drama happened at work today? How was your workout?" Conversations with my parents were great, but after sixteen months of living at home post-college, I realized they were a distraction—a distraction from sitting in silence with my own thoughts and feelings.

How does sitting in silence sound to you? Possible? Impossible?

Once I recognized the distraction, I tried to correct it and gain some clarity on my life. I'd try to sit and reflect, but after a few uncomfortable minutes, I'd let the noise of living with other people overwhelm me.

Still, I did as much as I could to carve out time for myself. And the more I slowly let myself enjoy my company alone, the more I realized I could experience those feelings daily if I lived in my *own* apartment. If I never created the opportunity to sit alone long enough, trying to control my thoughts and feelings for my benefit, I might still live with my parents.

If I stuck to my original plan, I could have moved out of my parents' house right after April 2020 when I paid off my last student loan—one month into a global pandemic.

I can hear myself probably saying, "Once the COVID-19 Pandemic *ends*, I'll start looking for apartments. Moving out makes little sense right now when the future is so unpredictable." I mean, as if anything pre-COVID-19 was ever predictable.

It's not that living with parents, siblings, or friends stops us from moving forward. It's the lack of letting ourselves enjoy our own presence, embracing silence, and letting our minds wander in ways that can help us move forward that keep us in the same place.

Once you learn how to sit with your thoughts, process the emotions and enjoy your own company, you'll have a process to eliminate distractions and make clear decisions. Knowing you can achieve clarity is one thing. Achieving clarity is another.

Often people will say they want to sit in their thoughts, but after a few uncomfortable minutes of silence, they'll default to letting those *damn distractions* take over.

What's distracting you from enjoying your own company? Could it be something you don't even realize is affecting you? Binging a Netflix series and telling yourself you need to finish the entire thing despite not even loving it? Saying yes to plans when people reach out simply to keep your calendar full and social life strong? Staying up late on dating apps hoping to find the one? Reminiscing about the past because you can't fully grasp your current reality?

After I moved out of my parents' house, I was in more control of my life than I'd ever been. When I wanted to turn the lights on or off and use the electricity I was paying for, I was the one who was in control to make the decision. I was *allowed to* control the heat, depending on my mood or feelings about where my money needed to be spent. I gave myself permission to work on side projects as much or as little as I wanted. I let myself lay down or have bummy days whenever I wanted because no one but me could decide what I did with my time.

I can still remember how great it felt to sit in my apartment during the first months on my own, eating healthy dinners *I made* for *myself*. When I eat well, though, I'm reminded why my decisions are so important. So now, I am trying.

For extroverts like me, social opportunities are one of my biggest distractions. Living alone meant I had no one to bounce ideas off right away. It was *only* me and my centered mind, which made creating habits and boundaries easier for me to follow through on. I grew to know how to walk away from people and situations that did not align with the life I wanted to live.

When someone would invite me out, I'd think; *Okay, will this interaction be worth 90 minutes and $45 of my life?*

If I hesitated to say yes, I wouldn't go. I got incredible at saying no to things that didn't fit my #DontWasteMyTime mentality.

Was saying no easy?

No.

Was it awkward?

Sometimes.

But I pushed through.

Saying no applied to all aspects of my life: people I'd known for years, people I'd just met, in social situations, and at work. And when I accepted an invitation, I'd leave as soon as *this is just a no for me dawg vibes* hit instead of *toughing it out* or feeling obligated. My brother taught me if your conversations with someone are *always* about other people, then you're around the wrong people. I put myself first. I love myself a solo Uber ride home.

We have the power to create these moments where we remind ourselves of our worth.

It wasn't until I moved into an apartment on my own that I began truly celebrating myself and my own worth. I was so myself that I only spent my time with those who were also themselves.

I started sharing about my new experience of living alone on social media when Instagram stories were the hot new thing.

"Danielle, I can't believe you're posting Instagram stories. It's so weird," friends would tell me who felt like Snapchat was still the *cool* place to be.

I used my Instagram stories to document the entire experience— finding my way on my own and living solo in an apartment. Since *every* penny mattered and I was so new to having rent and utilities expenses on my plate, I was constantly alone. Yet, it was the most unalone I've ever felt—not because I *wasn't* surrounded by people, but because I *was* surrounded by myself.

Living alone was one thing, but choosing to be alone was another. I was simply enjoying *my own* company—enjoying quieting my mind, reporting to no one but myself, making whatever decisions I wanted to make. I even found it difficult to go to work, not because I didn't love my job, but because I loved my apartment and what it opened up for me.

So fun. So alive.

I loved who I was, and I shared about it.

The power of conversation allows your mind to wander in a space where you can remind yourself of your thoughts and energy in the moment.

For the first time in my life, I did what I wanted to do because I could.

Seeing personal growth and success can be tracked holds an extreme amount of weight as opposed to just finishing a school paper and just being happy it's complete.

I made Instagram stories *cool* for myself and didn't care what anyone had to say about it. I made stories about me happily trying to figure out what the hell I was doing with my life, eating ramen day after day because I'd forget to go grocery shopping or putting my hair in a messy bun as I rocked sweaty gym clothes and Crocs at the grocery store.

I shared about how I talked to my pet hermit crab like he was my *only* friend.

One night, I had a few friends over and we were trying to get him to move into a new shell, but he wouldn't budge.

"Come on little dude, you got this!!!" We cheered. "Wait, what's his name again?" my friend Sawyer asked.

"Oh, I didn't name him," I said. "I didn't want to name him, become too attached, then get upset when he passed away. I don't trust myself to raise a hermit crab with a long life span."

"What? I'm gonna post a poll on my Instagram story to see what people think we should name him."

People started submitting names, and I felt excited for my hermit crab to have a stronger identity, one he deserved. One that felt more aligned.

They ended up naming him Chad, because what's a more bro name for a hermit crab than Chad.

Naming hermit crabs, businesses—just not my thing.

Within my first year in business, Sawyer posted a photo of her reppin' a Chylinski Media sweatshirt, logo big front & center, to her Instagram stories.

When I first started my business social media accounts, I updated the profile photo across platforms with a little drawing a friend made for me—a face, a bun, messy hair, glasses, with a smile—not realizing the impact it would have on my company, myself, and *everyone* in between.

The comfortable path would have been to wait until I figured out my branding before I posted anything. Instead, I believed my past would speak for itself when announcing my business, rather than relying on planned curated branding.

Anyway, so Sawyer's caption on her post read: "If Danielle saw me right now, she would say 'Bitch, go to the fucking gym.'"

So what did Sawyer do?

She went to the fucking gym.

The *distraction* of my giant face staring at her was enough for her to pause in her thoughts and make a move.

Not all distractions are bad. The delay of a distraction can create space for you to change your mind in a split second.

You *only* know what people choose to show you, not the 234567654 layers behind the post.

Sawyer could have *only* posted a photo of the sweatshirt with a "repping Chylinski Media in the gym" caption and tagged me. All of those who saw the post, including myself, never would have known she was trying to beat her procrastination struggle, or that my brand helped her push through. All we *would have* seen was her smiling face.

There's a reason Sawyer wanted them to know. She wanted to inspire those in her circle to push forward.

Life is about managing our reactions to our emotions. Emotions will forever change and evolve to create the new version of ourselves.

Just because I was posting random ass shit, someone is now repping my merch. Nothing really intentional was done to get her to do that. *That wasn't in the business plan*, mainly because there is no business plan LOL. I was posting because I liked to share my experiences in hopes someone could take a little of it with them on their journey, exactly how Sawyer had.

I never stopped posting Instagram stories; Not because I wasn't exhausted, or overwhelmed, or burned out, but because that's what kept me sane—what kept me, *me*.

During my hermit crab parenting era, I'd consistently get texts from friends and family asking if I was okay because with no direct communication about what I was up to, from an outside perspective, it looked like I was losing my shit and going through it while living alone—posting all hours of the day (sometimes reading at 3am) and sharing all random aspects of my life before it became more normalized like it is now. But from my perspective, *I was simply carefree.* I was doing what I wanted and not comparing myself to anyone else. I was trying new things, showing up however I wanted in the moment, experimenting with creating and holding boundaries, not asking for other people's opinions, and enjoying *my own* company and mind.

Honestly, I've never been better, I'd think whenever someone *worried* about me. That's where I want to be *every* day—so happy that not a single person understands how or why, and you owe them no explanation.

Getting to a place where you're fulfilled as an individual is overwhelmingly rewarding. Personal growth becomes so much clearer. Celebrating and acknowledging true growth doesn't happen often enough.

You first, *everyone else* second.

Being "alone," going places alone, was the most liberating feeling in the entire world. No one needed to know where I was, how I was, what I was doing. No one could tell me where or where not to be, how I needed to act, what I needed to do. *Only* I could.

I was alone, *not lonely.*

Sometimes being alone is an upgrade.

You get home, pour a glass of wine, sit on the couch, and there is silence. You get to decide if that's loneliness or freedom.

Alone time guides who you are as a person. Once you learn how to sit with your thoughts, process the emotions and enjoy your own company, making clear and aligned decisions becomes so much easier. You can feel like you're missing out, FOMO, when you're comparing. *Or* you can choose to see the opposite if you're making the decision solely on your personal happiness, JOMO—Joy Of Missing Out.

It wasn't until the COVID-19 pandemic, when we were all forced to be alone and sit in our thoughts, that we realized there are a lot of things we were happy to miss out on. While being alone wasn't necessarily a choice, once the world opened back up, many people began making decisions that were best for their needs, rather than societal needs.

We subconsciously think someone else has the answers for us, which often limits us from recognizing the options we have right in front of us. We quickly forget we have a choice around the reality we create.

One day during my senior year of college, I was sitting in my friend's dorm, talking with him and a few of his roommates about life after graduation.

"What type of job *should* I look for?" I asked their foreheads as they continued to scroll through their phones. There I was, a member of Student Senate and Class Council, a recipient of many leadership awards, as well as one of the top students in my Communication program, asking advice from guys who had no extracurricular experience, yet they all had jobs lined up before graduation.

In their silence, I realized no one held the answers for my future after graduation besides me. I no longer had the option to distract myself from putting in the work to understand my next move. I had to figure out who I was going to surround myself with after graduation—the people who were aligned with who I wanted to be. I decided enough was enough with that narrative—no more half-assed respect from my friends, classmates, colleagues, or family members. Wanting full respect and support, I wanted to give as much as I could in return.

Sometimes your people change, your needs change, your expectations shift, and you need to move away from certain people or situations and gravitate towards others. Take note, when you change and grow, of how you want to spend your time and who you want to spend it with. Many people don't know how this type of intentional decision-making feels.

Working on yourself is not selfish. It's not that you *only* care about yourself, it's that you want to be the best version of yourself for both yourself and for *everybody* around you. I shared a post to my Instagram story once that read, "Fuck nudes. Send me a dated invoice from your therapist so I know you're working on yourself."

Thoughts?

It's on you to make it clear what you expect for yourself so that you can avoid entering a state that does not serve you.

Choosing to happily exist as *you* should not feel like work.

You know what the real work is?

Building a life that doesn't serve you. *Building a life* trying to be like *everyone else*. *Building a life* that isn't authentic to you. Stop doing *that* work. Trying to be what *everyone else* wants you to be, that's work. Try keeping up with that... *No thank you.*

8. Energy Tells

How often do you go back and look at content you created and published?

When you do, you'll see how much you've grown while also experiencing shock from reflecting on where, and who, you used to be.

Okay, so I wasn't going to show you my college essay, but I have to show you. Please hold all negative opinions until you finish reading, LOL.

"Would you like a chocolate or vanilla twist? Sprinkles? Small, medium or large?" "Oh, no problem that your baby has chicken pox. I'll hold him." Welcome to an average day in my life, where I'm going out of my way to make customers ice cream at Dairy Queen as well as take notes and communicate with others at a Chiropractic office. From a sugary heaven where I'm covered in blizzard spray to noting subjective symptoms as I schedule adjustments, this is what I proudly call my life. I simply love my jobs. Sure, my parents would pay for my gas in a heartbeat and spot me twenty for the movies, but I like to work for my own money. It is the work ethic the women in my family have. This has been modeled by my mother and grandmother my entire life, I am not a stranger to hard work. They are strong and independent-painting, mowing, supporting, providing. That is what I learned and that is how I live my life.

If you're reading this like, "WTF Danielle?" Same girl, same.

The lack of awareness of the privilege I had as a teenager is scary to see now, so visible and concrete in my own words. I *expected* this essay to get me into college, which it did. However, I also *expected* this essay to reflect exactly who I was in under 400 words, which it didn't. Maybe it reflected who I was in the moment, but I had a bigger vision of what I believed my current reality to be.

My cringe worthy essay continued:

> *My friends ask me why I work two jobs, why I am so motivated; I tell them that it is in my nature, in my blood. I enjoy keeping busy and I love the sense of accomplishment I feel. When I take a moment to stand back and take a look at what I do on a daily basis, I feel awesome and even more energized! I have a positive attitude and I try to share that with people that I come into contact with at work, school or even at the mall! I just can't help sharing my belief that if you keep a positive attitude and mindset it will definitely take you places!*
>
> *Growing up seeing strong and independent women work for what they have has made me a driven person. Of course there are times that I have to work while my friends are playing mini golf or taking in the latest flick. I am proud of my accomplishments and my independence. So, whether I'm asking if someone wants strawberries, hot fudge or extra whipped cream or I am scanning a new patient's spine, I give it my all. That's just the way I work, no matter what environment: work, school or play. I work strongly academically just as much as I work hard for the customers I serve.*

If you wrote an essay like this and still have yours, look at it. Think about it. Did your essay fully reflect and embody who you were? Or are you like me saying, "LOL, wow this is the one sheet I trusted to get me into a college along with my not-so-hot transcript?" The "or even the mall!" part gets me.

I felt a sense of embarrassment to my core when I reread this essay recently. But, while writing it, I had strong supportive energy around me.

So how did this happen?

I would never speak like this ever in real life, so *why* was I writing this way? I mean, I'd argue that I didn't even write this. I relied on a lot of outside support to decide my words for me instead of believing in myself; I trusted these words to choose my fate.

I constantly tell my clients, "Write captions and text like you would say it out loud in-person. Otherwise, your words appears as weirdo robot vibes and not authentic at all. Use the voice-to-text feature so that the way you talk in real life translates smoothly."

We often think it's cringe to post, but you know what's cringier? Relying on someone else to find your voice and post on your behalf.

When we get stuck while writing, we think about who or what we trust to help us navigate our next step. Raise your hand if you've googled on average 657483945 grammar questions in your lifetime?

My hand is half raised because I grew up surrounded by many incredible family members who helped me. I'd call my Aunt Mari with grammar questions for a school paper and now, I occasionally ask for feedback on a podcast episode title.

When/if I have a baby though, I won't ask my Aunt Mari for feedback on a name LOL. She named her daughter (my cousin) Marianne, after my Grandma, MaryAnn.

Can you tell my family is a big fan of keeping names in the family?

If I have a kid, it seems like Danielle Lynn The Second is a potential option in the near future hahahahaha...

Anyway, sometimes I'd call my Mom too, but then her response might be, "Danielle, I don't have all the answers. Try YouTube or Google." She doubted herself as well once the questions got harder.

I never really choose to Google anything. I've basically lived my life forgetting Google exists, YouTube too, which some people would say *should* be illegal, but it's worked for me. Google may or may not fully understand the context, and doesn't give me a fair shot to explain myself in a fashion that it understands.

When my mom wasn't sure, I'd reach out to my grandma. My grandma is one of the kindest, smartest, happiest and most helpful people I know. Since elementary school, sometimes I'd call her as late as 10pm... Okay, maybe even sometimes 11pm.

"Hi Gram, can you help me with this writing assignment?" She'd *always* answer and help, no matter how late.

"Danielle, why are you waiting until B-E-D-time to start this?"

My grandma was a speech pathologist, owned her own practice for years, and was the first woman business owner in my family. I didn't know that until I started mine.

She definitely has played an impactful role on my confidence to do what I'm doing right this second. Even though now she says, "You're writing a book? Oh my gosh, Danielle. You're so smart and brave. I could never do that," I know she could.

Every day is a day for celebrating love, appreciation and respect for yourself, and making sure you're sharing time with the right people.

I tried, for years, in the beginning of college, to explain myself, to have my main group of girlfriends understand and respect what I was doing outside of hanging out with them, but they never did.

"You should stop by this event I'm hosting tonight. We've spent months planning it and it's going to be so fun. Free food, and even a DJ," I'd share with my roommates.

crickets

Or a sarcastic joke back like, "Sorry, I have plans to walk my pet hermit crab."

They'd disrespect my desire to be a part of clubs or campus events, and brush that part of me off like it didn't exist. But this part of me was fully who I was.

Why does it feel so hard to be supported?

"You don't necessarily do anything special, you just live what you say. You continue to take risks, following through on what *actually* brings you joy," a friend told me. "It's like the saying goes, do *you* think *you're* better than them, or do *they* think *you're* better than them, which subconsciously mirrors the lack of passion in their own life?"

I don't want you to love what I love. I want friends to respect me for the work I'm putting in, and not make excuses for why good things "happen" to me and not them.

I spent years chasing who I thought were my true actual friends, when in reality I had so many incredible friends right in front of me.

By Junior year, I had a private bedroom (so no direct roommate), within a suite of four girls. This was the most time I spent alone in college. My perspective quickly shifted on how and where I wanted to spend my time. I focused on those in front of me, and those who loved, supported and respected me for me. If I hadn't noticed the support from my "nerd friends," I never would have accepted positions or taken the steps to propel myself forward into the version of myself that proudly walked across the stage at my college graduation. Without these experiences, I may have never received the opportunity to speak in front of a large, powerful group of students.

A year after I graduated from college, an advisor I had in college invited me back to speak to the members of all the Student Executive Boards.

"Raise your hand if you post on your personal social media pages about what events you're hosting for the clubs you're a part of," I asked the audience.

Only two out of two hundred students raised their hands.

I followed up with, "How do you expect other people to support you when you're not supporting yourself?"

The audience became silent, staring back at me.

Have you ever done something silently, then felt frustrated when no one *supported* you the way you hoped they would? You need to be your biggest hype girl—not *only* for yourself but also for the missions and events that you strongly believe in. There are often people rooting for you, or trying to at least, and you may not even realize.

In college, my Student Senate advisor called me to her office.

"Danielle, I wanted to show you what another student wrote about you in their award application when asked to talk about a public figure that they look up to. Most people wrote about famous thought leaders, presidents, sports players, but someone wrote about *you*."

Me? I thought, shocked. I was reminded you never know who's watching or listening, and how you're affecting their life. *Someone wrote about me?*

If something isn't directly in front of us, we subconsciously forget about who else could be rooting for us.

Then again, other times, people might seem supportive in their actions, but their words might not align. Situations like this can turn you off, discourage you, and make you question your worthiness.

When I was working for the Hartford Yard Goats, I received an email from a former professor asking me if I would come back and speak to her class.

I immediately responded. "Yes, 100%!"

I used my PTO and took a day off work to volunteer, traveled over an hour, and spoke for 90 minutes to a class of upcoming Communication —Public Relations undergraduate students. I could feel them soaking up my enthusiasm and excitement. It felt incredible to give back and inspire students to have hope for what their degree could do for them.

The students thanked me one-by-one as they walked out the door at the end of the presentation.

When the professor and I were the *only* two people left, we walked into the hallway together.

"Great job!" She told me. "You know, though, you *only* got your job because you're pretty. You can't tell people about your journey and leave out the part where your looks got you where you are."

Excuse me? I thought, dumbfounded. I laughed the comment off in the moment, but my heart hurt as I walked away. *This professor is the woman who had taught one of the most impactful classes during my undergraduate career. I admired her for years and valued her opinion. She saw the smile on my face and how happy I was to share about my journey after college. Why didn't her words make me feel like she was proud of me?*

When our worth is questioned, or laughed at because someone *above us, higher than us, older than us, or more experienced than us,* attempts to quantify it, we may catch ourselves laughing because we're uncomfortable.

A woman I went to college with, Ryann, reached out to me for help in the middle of the pandemic after her wellness coaching *failed*.

"I started a six-week program in October and had 5-6 clients drop out last minute," she explained. "I've been struggling with the two clients I have."

It made me so happy because this was someone who had recognized the support she already had in her corner, reached out and asked for help.

"Prior to reaching out to you, I've been trusting a *stranger* for help I found through a sponsored Instagram post."

After speaking with me, though, she quickly saw the value of someone she knew giving her pure love, direct support, and no bullshit.

"I want to talk through what I've been doing and why it's not working. I need to find alternative ways to make my business *more successful*, and determine how I can use social media in a more effective way to increase engagement and interest."

"Love it, let's do it! I think doing six biweekly phone calls for 30 minutes each to start would be most effective. Thoughts?"

"Sounds perfect. I'm so ready. When can we start?" Ryann said back to me, with a giant smile on her face.

On our first call, she shared, "Wow, I know we're *only* halfway into this phone call, but I seriously feel it's already been more valuable than that other multiple-month-program I paid for."

I was impressed, but not shocked. There is support all around you and sparks happen when you reach out to them.

"That's incredible. I'm so happy you find this so helpful. Take a minute and think about *who else* you may possibly overlook in your network? *Who else* could you talk to on a deeper level? It takes courage to be open to seeing how much support you have in your network and really allowing it in, but all it takes is one conversation," I said back to her.

Full circle—Ryann was the one my advisor told me about, the one who wrote about me in their award application. Four years later, here I was, honored to help and support her business.

9. Disrespect Doesn't Live Here

"I used to go to school to escape home," Mia told me the first time we met. "But now I go home to escape school."

I was supposed to be telling her about the day-to-day in my job, but as a Junior in high school—laughing, eye rolling, shaking her head while being choked up, confused, let down and frustrated—she opened up to me about her reality.

"School is supposed to be a place where you feel safe," she said. "I feel bad for students younger than me. It's *only* going to get worse."

Feeling exhausted and overwhelmed from being bullied and disrespected, as well as from her drive to 'go viral' on social media so she could be 'cool' and accepted, she seemed hopeless. She was extremely aware of what was going on around her, yet unsure who she could trust to talk about her experiences.

I *met* Mia *only* minutes before.

About five of the front office staff were presenting to a group of students about our job responsibilities.

I listened to my colleagues, one by one, share their experience.

"I'm Joe. I've been working here for 8 years. My major in college was history. I know wild, right? How did I end up in sports?"

"Hi, my name is Corey. I work in sponsorship. I love interacting with the community."

"Sup, I'm Tay. I'm born and raised in Connecticut. I interned here for a year before they asked me to be a full-time employee."

Then, it was my turn.

"Raise your hand if you like baseball. Raise your hand if you've been to a Yard Goats game. Raise your hand if you've never been to a game. Raise your hand if you wish you've been to a game. My job is to figure out how to get *every single person* in this stadium for a game—date night, girls night out, a school trip, a family night. My goal when posting consistently on social media is to target each type of person from *every* demographic with *every* possible thought in mind—with the intention of getting them in the ballpark. Don't like baseball? Don't care. Here are some other things you can do at Dunkin' Donuts Park rather than watch the game. I could care less if they watch the game. I just want them to be excited to come here and have an awesome time with people they love."

The highschool students stared back at me like; *The fuck? Did you really just say you don't care if they watch the game?*

"What you may not know is that Minor League Baseball, from my position, is more of an entertainment industry than a sports industry. The goal for us *every* day is to entertain our community."

The groups of students were still shocked, looking at me like; *Yo, when is this chick's boss gonna step in?* But my male coworkers stood behind me, smiling, nodding their heads, supporting what I was sharing.

The last speaker shared his background, and then we broke for lunch. During that time, the students were tasked to rank each of the Front Office staff members using a scale from 1 to 5—1 being the person they wanted to spend the rest of the day shadowing and 5 being the person with the job they least wanted to learn more about. Each student would *only* be selected for one shadow opportunity.

The director of the event pulled me aside. "Danielle, wow, you were a popular one among the students. A majority wanted to spend more time with you, but we had to spread them out among the other staff." She laughed a little and smiled at me.

I smiled back, surprised but not surprised at all.

I made my way to the conference room, waiting for the few students selected to meet with me to come in. It ended up being four of us, me and three highschool girls. The point of meeting with the students 1:1 in a small group was for them to ask me about my job, but really they just wanted my opinion on how they could *survive* their high school experience.

Truly connecting with someone means your *self is going out*, then remaining open so other people can connect back with you.

I want to help people who want help. Some people are satisfied with blaming those around them (or other external factors), taking zero ownership, while others truly want to live a better life.

On this day, I was Mia's unexpected resource. By simply asking questions and listening, she realized I was engaged in the conversation with her. Within minutes, the walls were down, and she opened up about her reality. As we parted ways, Mia turned to me and said, "I just shared more with you in a few hours than I have with most people in my entire life. Thank you."

Sometimes people just *need* to be heard. Sometimes that's the most powerful thing we can do. Why are we so afraid to see other people as they are?

Honestly, I think we are so afraid because we resist seeing ourselves in our truth.

A few of my best friends were also in that fake marketing pitch course I had to take, including my direct dorm roommate, Emilie (the one I visited in Florida)—direct, as in her bed was literally feet away from mine in the same room. Direct. We were in the second semester of our Senior year, so at this point our toes touched for over 5 months.

One day, we were going over our assigned readings as a class, with the professor asking questions to see how well we understood the material. It's safe to say I didn't have many correct answers, but I had a lot of questions. However, I was *always* down for attempting to answer.

"Danielle, what are your thoughts about the chapter you read for homework last night?" The professor asked.

I'm thinking about how I did not read, so I have absolutely no idea. I also tried to read the chapter from last week but it was so unclear so I don't even know how to lie right now... I had no idea what the answer was, mainly because I was having trouble even understanding the question.

When I gave my best shot of an answer, Emilie couldn't hold back a laugh. The definition of Laughing Out Loud. A loud laugh, one she couldn't contain. No one else in the class laughed. *Only* Emilie.

Rather than getting *awkward or embarrassed in my skin* for answering wrong and having her laugh at me, I was *awkward and embarrassed for her.* I was well aware I had no idea what I was saying, and it wasn't the answer the professor was looking for, but I was proud of myself for responding and engaging in the conversation like I normally do.

After all, school is for learning, not for schooling the teacher or the rest of the class.

I gave Emilie no attention or a reaction to anyone in the class. I let her have her moment to shine. She did what she felt she needed to, and I simply sat there. This was a big learning moment for me. I realized I loved to be confidently *wrong.* I was proud of having contributed to the discussion rather than saying I don't know. I would never laugh at someone for having the wrong answer, especially someone so close to me and in a public setting.

When people do things like this, recognize it's not a reflection of you. It's a reflection of them. More than likely, they're hurting. Hurt people hurt people.

When you're on that HFD, high-flying disc (Google it), you're not hurting people. You're not even in a place where you're capable of hurting anyone because you are so in love with who you are, what you stand for, and what you are doing.

As a millennial, I think it's *pretty damn clear* we will not put up with the way things "are" or how they were when our parents grew up. I mean, rightfully so, considering each generation lived a different lifestyle and had different expectations. We like to address situations that don't work. Not *only* do we address them, but we analyze them and try to understand and determine how we can improve situations. Millennials and the generations to come aren't putting up with the half-assed respect. We are here for positive work environments, meaning a place to spend our time where we feel strong and confident within ourselves. If it's not provided to us, we'll create our own with the awareness that we're in control of our time and decisions.

Think back to the 9-5 model and how it began with factory workers —men doing the same mindless task over and over, while women stayed home. Then, the same hourly model applied to people doing extremely strenuous mental tasks. That was 100 years ago.

No amount of disrespect is worth your time. Make room for the right people to walk into that open spot—whether that's a new employer, client, or friend. *You have to make open spots, though.*

By saying no to being disrespected, you'll be leaning into the full control you have over your life and allowing something fulfilling to consume your days. Settling for disrespect sends a message of how you let people treat you. You don't have to convince anyone of anything. If you stand by your decision, then the *consequences* on the other end don't matter.

When I founded Chylinski Media, I was already helping people with their social media accounts in various aspects. The more I helped, the more I wanted to help. It didn't take long before I was shifting my business from managing accounts to consulting others on how they can better manage their accounts from a place of intuition and intention organically, helping them *look* as good online as they do in person—how they show up, tone of voice, font choices, post frequency, responses to DMs and much more.

Social media isn't something that can genuinely be passed off, followed by a celebratory "yay, checked that off the list." Social media is meant to be social. It's easy to run away and avoid your emotions, but if you want to feel good about yourself, you need to lean in. Once you show up as yourself, it's not about "needing to post." It's about feeling excited to engage in conversation with other human beings.

In the early stages of building Chylinski Media, I had a lot of lessons to learn.

Gaining clients exclusively through referrals, though, allowed the anxiety to be less up front. As a business owner, it's an honor when you get referrals. The person referring you is saying, "I trust this person with what she says she can do, and then some. Work with her. She's your girl."

And often clients say, "I have no idea what I need or want, but know I'm in the right place by talking to you." It's not *always* about the services you offer. It's the fact that *you* are the one offering these skills.

"I think about how much I need to increase my social media presence, being true to myself, and not making it feel like a chore, but it feels so far out of reach and impossible to commit to," potential clients share day after day. Except I'm right here with open arms saying *let's do it*. Don't waste any more time *not doing it*.

I quickly became exhausted by spending so much time talking with someone, just to find out we did not align—I realized I was the problem, not them. Open communication, understanding where your client's head is at, and focusing on the *whys* is important. There is no fakeness and no awkward boundaries, *only* facts and feelings.

A prospective client isn't *always* a good fit for you; they may not match your expectations, communication style, or boundaries. When you encounter someone struggling in an area of your expertise, your natural instinct is to step in and help.

With one of my referrals, the prospective client was the founder of a new marketing startup who needed help to establish all new social media accounts and branding assets. I agreed to an initial consultation with Madelyn to learn more about her and her company, and to discuss how I might help.

When I met Madelyn in person, for some reason, she had already set up a company email address for me, and told me she would pay me $200 a week.

A week.

She *expected me* to travel three hours out of state at least twice a week.

"This is a full-time position," Madelyn told me.

I still knew nothing about her company.

What the actual fuck; I thought. *The only communication we've had was literally her asking to meet up to see if I'd be a good fit. I don't even know the name of her company or what industry she's in. Why the hell has she set me up as a full-time employee? None of this makes sense.*

Blind-sided going into the meeting, I thought I was going to be leading a conversation with a potential new client for my business. I was so shocked to the point where I *somehow* accepted her offer. I couldn't find my words.

When I got home, I immediately rambled a recount of the situation to my boyfriend. "*Just* send her an email," he said.

How could I "just" send her an email? I had to explain why I couldn't help, why I was backing out of the situation. I'm not a quitter. I don't give up, but I wanted to play by my rules, not hers. I stand behind who I am: a businesswoman who wants to help.

After a few weeks of being lost, feeling out of control and trying to figure out how to handle the situation, I sent Madelyn this email:

After understanding more of what you're looking for, I've decided I'm not a good fit for this role. I've realized I cannot commit to an hourly schedule right now, and I am focusing my needs and attention on building my business, my new goals and environment. I've been trying to be adaptive, but it's been difficult. I haven't been myself because I can't fully commit, and it hasn't been fair to you. I'm learning a ton, but my path is definitely building my company and serving my small business clients on a much smaller scale. I feel you would benefit from someone who can better organize, manage, allocate more time, and be located closer in proximity to you. While I know we've achieved a lot in a short amount of time, and you're working on building a larger team to conquer and divide, I'm not sure I'm that person long term and don't feel it's fair to continue. If you want to contract me through my LLC to do minor projects directly related to social media pages and graphics, we could talk about that. I'd be happy to assist for the next two weeks and continue to get you organized and do housekeeping tasks until you have more of a team in place. I'll send an overview from this week today or tomorrow. Let's pick a time on Monday to talk!

Madelyn replied, "Send over all passwords and any documents."

I sent over what she asked, and she never responded again.

Madelyn took advantage of me because she recognized I was a new business owner still learning the ropes, yet passionate to help others. Looking back, this whole situation would not have existed if I held my boundary of a 15-minute consultation call. *The call I chose to have in person rather than virtual* because I respected the woman who referred me.

This is why it's important to pause and reflect. It's easy to get carried away in situations like this. I used this experience to grow, learning to help people while still respecting my own time and boundaries.

Another past client once told me, "There's no way you spent 15 hours a week on this work," after I sent over my monthly timesheet and invoice.

I thought to myself; *I told you I'd do 15 hours of work for you a week. I probably did another ten hours of work that I was nice enough not to bill you for. Yet you're questioning my integrity?*

Situations like these are tough. One factor we can try to control is our communication style.

As work and personal life moved more online, the two blended together. Creating new parameters around what I can tolerate and what I will not tolerate—mentally, physically, and emotionally—in my communication was a must.

Setting boundaries for how you communicate is crucial.

Boundaries = self respect.

Recognize what your personal communication style is and pay attention to the communication styles of the people who you're working with.

In a local TV interview on NBC Connecticut, I provided an entire breakdown of how determining communication expectations can make or break your interactions. Consider saying explicitly what your style is and asking others their style so you're both clear about what to expect from each other. There isn't enough conversation about our different styles and how we operate best.

Some people are comfortable with late-night texts. Others are fine answering phone calls on the weekend. Many aren't.

"Oh my gosh, so and so texted me about a work thing at 9:00pm. Can you believe it?"

They might complain, roll their eyes, text someone else to talk shit, and hold it against you.

While providing services or doing excellent work is your full-time job, commanding respect is a part-time job if you want to remain in control and not settle for less than you deserve. Learning to be strong enough to disappoint people (saying yes or no) in a way that serves you most is a skill you can learn.

Be kind to yourself. Take breaks from communicating if it feels like way too much. Ignore that text message instead of responding within minutes of receiving, or let that email sit in your inbox unread over the weekend and read it on Monday. You are allowed to do that; you're not a bad person, friend, coworker, family member or business owner if you don't drop *everything* for *everyone else* literally 24/7/365. Respect yourself by setting boundaries that put *you* first. Continue to make promises to yourself and *honor them.*

I'm not *always* sure where disrespect comes from and lives, but it sure as hell is not in my presence.

10. Connect Like a Human (Please)

CaN i PiCk YouR BrAiN?

Please don't. That doesn't seem like it would feel good. Nothing about being asked by someone if they can pick my brain sounds like something I want to be a part of. My brain immediately self-destructs when someone says this to me. How did I respond the last time someone slid into my DMs on LinkedIn and asked?

"Sure," I told Jason. "This falls under a business strategy call on my Chylinski Media service list. Here's the link with more information. Let me know if this serves as something you're interested in and I can send over some dates and times for a call next week!"

"Just so I understand," Jason replied. "I'm paying for your time to share ideas?"

As soon as I saw the message my instant thought was *Fuck you, dude. What?! I'm so exhausted by giving so much of my brain for free constantly. It's mentally exhausting, literally.* But I assumed as a business owner I couldn't ignore or tell someone straight up, "Fuck you," so I asked a business owner friend what she thought would be more appropriate response. She sent me a draft, and without much thought, I copied and pasted it word for word, and sent it back to Justin.

"Correct. That is consulting, which is a service I offer as the owner of Chylinski Media. In business strategies calls, we break down what your business concept is together, ask the hard questions to dig deeper in your mission, and leave you with helpful action steps to think about.

This is done with my marketing experience and expertise regarding what we can implement to increase your reach, revenue, etc. through communication, public relations, and social media strategies."

No reply from Jason.

If I got his message today, I would literally have instantly responded and said, "Fuck off."

Just kidding; I wouldn't have replied.

I was clearly feeling some type of way, but I had to take a step back and react with logic instead of emotion. *Which is not always easy.*

It's not *always* easy to manage messages like these or your emotions when they hit you hot. As someone who used to normally respond *disgustingly timely* and felt the need to please *everyone* immediately, it takes practice to change your habits.

Anyway, I'm not saying asking a stranger for advice is wrong. I just strongly believe there are more respectful ways other than *CaN i PiCk YouR BrAiN?* to start a conversation that would imply the same thing but create a more human, social, empathetic, two-sided connection.

It's easy to assume others have the same intentions as you. After being burned enough times though, I have my boundaries set. Walls are up high, baby.

"We *should* grab coffee soon. I'd love to pick your brain about a few things!"

"I'd love to talk strategy about captions."

"I'm curious about your opinion on which platform I *should* spend my time on."

"Let's set up a Zoom call and catch up."

What all these comments *actually* mean is *I need help and I think you may be able to.*

Lots of *shoulding* all over the place. *What does Danielle want rather than feel like what she should do?*

Sometimes the person asking needs help with something as small as what they *should* wear for a presentation. Other times, they need help with something as big as figuring out what they're passionate about.

What they're saying is, "I respect your opinion, and I'd love to know more about what it is and why."

That makes me wonder—who else is thinking the same thing and who else has the same questions?

I love talking to people one-on-one because, more and more, people are giving themselves permission to be vulnerable, and they're opening up and expressing their honest thoughts. We can sit in a coffee shop and listen to each other one-on-one, but often the conversation is something meaningful that the entire coffee shop *also* needs to hear. I've left so many conversations mad at myself because with so much great information shared, I *knew* other people would benefit from being at that table. I felt like such strong conversations were going to *waste* by not being amplified. I wanted to talk more publicly so a larger audience could find value.

To spotlight the power of conversation, I launched my podcast, Coffee Date with D in December of 2020.

In my intro, I explain: "I have left so many authentic conversations like, wow, that was so good—I wish I had recorded that. What I've learned through connecting one-on-one is the value of being vulnerable and honest in expressing your thoughts. Get ready for unfiltered mini rants, allowing our minds to wander and open up to new ways of thinking. I'm your host, Danielle Chylinski, founder of Chylinski Media, and this is the power of speaking your truth into existence."

Oversharing about who you are or what you're doing or thinking is a fear people have. But that's often because you *actually* fear the idea of execution, lacking confidence in yourself to execute accordingly to bring your vision to life. I strongly believe if you choose to not execute something, there is a reason you're not. You are consciously deciding to make certain decisions daily to avoid executing, whether or not you realize it. And a decision to not do something as opposed to doing nothing is *still* a decision.

Take responsibility for what's happening in your life. *Only* you feel the exact way you feel in that moment. If you're not happy with it, how do you need to change so you can become your best and most authentic self? Do you need to have more conversations? Different kinds of conversations? Conversations with different people?

I delayed creating the Coffee Date with D podcast for a long time because I made excuses—*it would be one more thing added to my to-do list.* I didn't know how I was going to be consistent about putting out new episodes. But just like the thought of moving out of my parents' house got stuck in my head, eventually I hit a point where the idea for this podcast was in my head *every* day, *every* hour, *every* minute. I realized, *so what* if I'm not as consistent as I want to be? *So what* if it adds more to my workload and I have to make adjustments?

So here I am, hosting a podcast because it needs to be out in the world for me to be at my peak state, for me to be *me*, for myself and for those around me. It is about getting conversations out into the world that I feel people can learn and benefit from. No one ever has the same conversations that I do, just as no one has the same conversations that you do.

Sometimes people don't like to share raw things. They hit *post* or *publish* or *send* only once their message or content feels *perfect*. With that comes many missed opportunities for people to grow and learn together. Many people are struggling behind closed doors because they don't know who to go to for help (including me sometimes). People try to give the impression that they have it together.

Honestly, I'm not impressed. I'm exhausted. One of the best things I learned and kept in the back of my mind, especially as a business owner, is that no one *actually* knows what they're doing. *Like seriously, no one knows.*

We're all doing our thing, trying to show how cool, calm, and collected we are, while dealing with constant imposter syndrome.

This happened to me when presenting to college students in a marketing class. The host said, "Danielle! You're a new CEO and business founder. That's incredible. Tell us more!"

I fumbled for a response. "Oh, um, me, yeah, hi. I guess that is me. Yes, I'm an owner and a founder."

It still gets awkward sometimes. The weight of being a business founder holds a lot of value in the public eye, and it makes you question yourself daily—not *only* whether you'll be able to make your business a success, but also *who you are as a person.* The more struggle I experience, the more confident I am in calling myself a business founder.

I realized I am the founder of *being myself,* just like you, too, are the founder of being yourself.

I am me.

You are you.

So many people will never understand, or get close to themselves because they aren't willing to share who they are until they look the "best they can" on the outside.

Who are you on the inside? You don't have *everything* together or look shiny and perfect, but embrace it. This is what it means to have a personal brand, whether or not you own a business.

For years now, I've said yes to sharing my story and creating space to do so. Often, a lot of our failures and successes can look like they just happened overnight or came naturally. This has made me want to share my experiences as often as I can. No one will ever know all the work that went into an outcome. The vulnerability I've allowed for myself, by myself, has given me the strength of consistent, deep reflection. I'm open about how people and experiences have affected me. Some of my stories may not be easy to share in the moment but, eventually, I share. For me, there are no secrets to why I'm *unapologetically me.*

I'm still trying to untangle how I got here. Maybe I was just too lazy to Photoshop my photos when it became popular, or I didn't feel like going the extra step to over-whiten my teeth before I posted. I learned it was much easier and satisfying to be myself than to share this fake "better than myself" image with the world, and to compete with those who were trying to share their own "better than themselves" images.

Why do we deem certain posts "Instagram worthy" presenting this perfect (*false*) image of ourselves to the world of perfection?

Denying, rejecting or hiding parts of yourself can get uncomfortable. You're worthy the way you are—*your entire identity.*

Put your own mini-rants out into the world, allowing people into your mind for an opportunity to understand your way of thinking. Show that it's okay to not have it all together, but still share where you're at in life. It's cool to be like, *WHAT THE FUCK IS GOING ON*, and to be open to the idea that some days are incredible while other days you never want to leave your bed.

Coffee Date with D isn't for people who have it together; it's for people who just want to talk as people. Share what we're passionate about. Talk about what we contribute, bring to the table and what we feel confident, or not so confident about. What messages we want or may not want to share with the world, but we're going to do it, anyway. It is an open floor for conversation. By hearing what someone is saying and listening to the emotion that comes along with it, we can grow so much stronger *together*.

I speak my mind; you speak yours. We'll back it up with facts and feelings without second guessing the words we're putting into existence. Let's walk away from our conversations, feeling good about ourselves and what we said. No one can say your feelings are invalid or that facts are not facts. *Facts.*

Acknowledge our different ways of thinking and recognize the power of letting our ideas live freely out loud. When you talk out loud, your mind wanders; suddenly your thought feels complete and *more real.* You may end up saying something from deep within you didn't realize was even there. Bouncing ideas off someone else allows us to fully create a complete thought about something. Through that, we'll realize the answers are often already within us. We know a lot more than we give ourselves credit for.

You never know who's listening, or who can benefit from what you're doing or have already done. Each of us has a story to tell and experiences to share that someone out in the world is waiting to hear— whether they know it or not.

Whenever I speak to a potential client, they end up spilling their hearts out to me. It starts with a version of them being so fed-up with themselves.

"I seriously want to commit to getting my social media accounts looking as great as I feel in person."

They tell me what they want, how much they want it, how badly, how often they think about it, how they'll do whatever it takes, and how excited they are that our paths crossed.

Naturally, I feel the excitement too. *I'm excited for them* because they want this badly. I'm *excited for myself* because I get to help them through this transformation. I write and send over a proposal, expecting a quick response. But, sometimes I never hear back. Ghosted.

I received a DM on Instagram from two women who had recently started a business: "Someone sent me your name. We're in desperate need of a logo ASAP. Let me know when we can hop on call."

I didn't answer the same day as I normally would because I never got a notification that would have prompted me to accept the message request. The sender was *so committed* and interested in working with me that, when they didn't receive a quick reply from me, they went out of their way to email me, too.

YAAAAASSSS, I thought to myself when I saw the email. *Let's go!!!!!!!!*

When we got on a call, they said they needed a logo for their business as soon as possible so they could order business cards. They had a vision, but they needed someone to bring it to life for them—and they believed the person was me.

I could hear the stress and urgency in their voices. "We're going to send you some designs we've drawn on a napkin. I really hope you can recreate this. We have clients already waiting for our services. We just need to lock in our logo and branding."

Since they were committed to me, I was beyond excited to collaborate with these two strong women business owners. I gave them a rough estimate of what the pricing would be over the phone and added, "We'll revisit the final number once the project wraps up."

Unlike my social media services, creating a logo was one of my secondary services so I hadn't finished all the backend details yet.

"Amazing," they agreed. "Sounds good. Thank you so much!"

We got right to work. We had multiple phone calls, and I mocked up a bunch of design options for them. I completed their dream logo in less than a week, putting in over twelve hours of work. Normally, this type of project would take about a month.

I finalized and converted the logo into several file types, designed their brand book with the logo colors and fonts, as well as highlighting what sparked the inspiration.

"Once I receive payment," I notified them via email, "I'll send over all the files."

No response. I called, texted, and emailed. *No response.* After a week of consistent communication and interaction with them... Ghosted.

Eventually, they began replying to my text messages. Each time, they had a different excuse for the payment delay.

"We're waiting on the legal confirmation of our LLC."

"We're waiting for our bank accounts to complete their setup."

"We're waiting for our credit card to come in."

And still no payment.

I wasted my time. I *thought* these women were genuine and as excited to dive into their business as I was for them. I *assumed* their vision and their integrity matched mine. I obviously wasn't thinking; *why would I do this work without making sure I received payment before we started any work?*

Now, I only do work for clients when being paid upfront. I have a habit of loving people *more than* they love themselves; I often see a deeper version of them than their current self. When I fall in love with your business' potential more than you, that's when I let myself down, naturally.

I've learned quickly, everyone's urgency is not your emergency.

While I could look at this disaster of an experience as a loss, I choose to look at it as a reminder of #DontWasteMyTime.

While your intentions and thoughts come from a good place, people you consider working with might not align in the same ways. Build in a system that works for you—whether in business or your personal life—and stick to it with intention. Happiness can still come for you, and it will continue if you're playing by your rules.

To this day, they have not paid me. I survived, though, and I'm often reminded of scenarios like these when I cash a client check bigger than my old monthly salary.

Like how the fuck did I get here?

But, I've learned a lot through the process, been through some shit and grew from many experiences. I got my *hot girl glow* back because I *chose* to bring it back rather than letting people who didn't value me take that away from me.

Expectations

Learning how to manage your expectations of others can help you better understand what is stopping or distracting you from prioritizing yourself. You may often put others' needs before your own—why?

11. Doesn't Serve You? Walk Away

If you're *always* waiting for the *perfect* time to execute, you'll never execute. The perfect time does not exist—really it's any time you want, like ever.

I created Chylinski Media once I realized how many people I supported to embrace themselves online. I started off bartering, and that was great—but I wanted to change my response from, "Just buy me a coffee or something" to "I'll send you an invoice." I wanted Chylinski Media to be the resource for people who felt I could help them with their branding needs, without feeling awkward about asking. I never intended the business to be something I actively promoted, but rather something I would mention if the right opportunity came up.

Chylinski Media to be a career choice? Never an intention either, nor did I ever think it would be possible. But, when the possibility of turning it into a career presented itself, I went for it.

I'm going to file for an LLC; I committed to myself. I didn't know who to trust to help me with the next steps after spending countless hours brainstorming about naming my business, but I knew I was going to have my own company.

My notebook filled up with possible names, phrases, words, ideas, thoughts, and drawings—but I couldn't decide. Starting a business seemed impossible; *It seemed too official.* After all, these decisions would go on legal documents.

When I called my lawyer, I was upfront with her. I shared I had absolutely no idea how to register for an LLC and was struggling to decide on the name. My first strong thought was; *This company has to have Chylinski in it because my name is my brand and credibility.* Yet, each time I told someone I was going to start an LLC, guess what they told me?

"Whatever you do, make sure your last name isn't in it in case you get married and *have* to change it."

When I started the business, I was Danielle Chylinski. I *am still* Danielle Chylinski. I may not *always* see that, but that's exactly what others see. So why would I not own who I am in the present moment fully? The more I realized people don't remain present and purpose-fully shy against it, the more I knew I needed to be louder about why I choose to. So many of the choices I've made and things I've done were predictable for *me* to make—that's what friends, family, and colleagues mean whenever they've said, "That's so Danielle Chylinski of you."

I'm consistent at least, huh?

Learn how to stop "becoming" and to start being.

When would the people in your life say, "That's so *insert your name* of you?"

Chylinski Media was a social media marketing and brand identity company, and I was telling people I could help them with their social media and branding without even having any of my own when I first launched. On the surface, it makes no sense.

But, hey, I already had clients based on the strength of my own personal brand.

For me, having a business plan floating in the air (nothing on paper) was better than having no company. Nothing (or anything, really) was in place, and I continued to learn as I went.

I don't have the time to be haunted by the what ifs.

I'm working in a field where I give people permission to be confident and comfortable in being themselves, to do what they want, think what they want, and feel what they want.

"Yeah, Danielle I want to post more consistently but I *just can't.*"

"Well, let me tell you a hundred reasons why I think you can."

I do that through speaking my truth and reminding people, like you, the importance of doing what you want, because it makes you feel good about yourself.

Why couldn't I do that for myself when naming my business? I'm often able to explain things to others by taking away their distorted view of how "they're supposed to do things." I deserved that for myself, too.

Great things never come from staying in your comfort zone, and I knew I needed to continue on the path of creating and maintaining a life I couldn't wait to wake up to—continuing to be consciously aware of what I want and don't want, and why it is such a large piece of my life.

How much of the stuff in your head that you're telling yourself is *actually* true?

We often forget the most important thing: loving and finding happiness within ourselves.

It's not the easiest journey, but once you get there, you want nothing more than to stay there. You create and decide your reality. The feeling of happiness is something you choose. It doesn't happen to you, or find you. It's an emotion you decide to feel.

I've never been able to rely fully on someone else's opinion. I like to make my own without it being tampered too much by external factors, especially a factor such as "likes."

When you're succeeding, what's going on? I can sure as hell tell you it's not from you chillin' in your comfort zone.

You are in control of your time, how you want to spend it, and who has the privilege of spending it with you. We get distracted and forget that we own our time. Whether you own your own business or you work for a large corporate company or nonprofit, you are still in control and you don't need to let anyone run your time.

I have a client who constantly talks about the same five people. "They're not looking to put in the work to grow or change, they're only looking to talk (complain)." It does nothing for either of them, besides steal my client's passion, joy and happiness around his business.

Six months later, he's still doing the same thing—same excuses.

"I have no time."

"My whole day is suddenly gone. I never have time to post."

"It's exhausting. How do people live life like this?"

You're choosing to live your life with them; I thought to myself.

"This is on you now." I said back. "This is your responsibility. Take ownership of your reality or walk away from it. Regardless, the choice is yours. No one said it would be easy."

If you are letting people control your time, not *only* are you hurting yourself, but you're also hurting the people you're *working* with.

12. Speak Up

On my first day of working in MiLB, I walked to my desk and thought; *Oh no, a desktop computer. How the fuck am I going to work? I haven't used a desktop since the college library.*

The next thought that went through my head was; *I need a laptop. Not just any laptop. I need a MacBook. I need to AirDrop.*

In the back of my mind, I knew I had to figure out how to ask for a MacBook.

After a few months, and a thousand different scenarios I ran through my head, I finally pulled all my mental notes together. All I had to do was build up the courage to ask my boss, Cameron, for what I knew I needed to be the best I could at this job.

When I finally found the courage to ask Cameron, he told me to ask the president, Jake, directly.

Fuckkkkkk.

I got up from my desk, walked down the hall, and shot my shot.

"I was wondering if I can get a laptop, specifically a MacBook laptop?"

Jake asked, "Why?"

"Having a laptop will help me be the most efficient I can be at my job, which would then translate to what I produce daily and the success of the company. Between photos, messages, and notes, AirDrop's speed in sharing information is unparalleled and could save hours of unnecessary work. Without it, doing basic tasks will take 10x longer."

A few days later, I walked into the office. Sitting on my desk was a silver MacBook Air with a mint green case, courtesy of the president.

Once other employees noticed, they started talking.

"Wait, what? How'd you get a laptop?"

"I asked and explained why I needed it. I built my case for how it'll help my workflow and outcome, and how that would be better, overall, for the company."

Slowly, I *became* the person others reached out to when they needed to ask for something they knew would help them execute their job better.

"I'm too far into the job," my coworker Blair said. "I can't ask now."

So not true. Why would you choose to feel less than and uncomfortable every day? What's the worst that can happen? They say no?

Sometimes managing your expectations of other people also means managing expectations of yourself. I remember telling myself; *damn Danielle. You can't expect you out of everybody else.*

If I had never opened my mouth about the desktop computer, I might have developed strong negative feelings that would take over my day.

Wow, how can he not see I need a MacBook to make my life easier? If he was smart, he'd know getting me one would help the overall revenue of the company.

I could have spent day in and day out complaining to my coworkers, friends, and family about how hard my job was because I had to use this unhelpful desktop computer. Instead, I pushed through, took a risk, and stopped myself from creating a limiting belief that wasn't true.

Have you ever been on the receiving end of an incorrect assumption based on a role or environment you were in?

People often expect you to act a certain way, be a certain person, or hold a certain view. These spoken (or unspoken) expectations can make being the current version of yourself difficult. You become stuck in the real-time battle of expectations versus reality.

"Oh, you work in sports? This experience must be incredible as a sports fan. Who's your team?"

How much *I love sports* somehow *always* managed to make it into a conversation with someone I just met. Whether they're decked out in team gear, program in hand, and the roster memorized (including stats) or someone I'm having a random conversation with while in line at a coffee shop, it's all the same. What these fans don't realize is, just because you work in sports doesn't mean you love sports or even know the sport inside and out.

"I don't know what that acronym stands for."

"I don't have a favorite team."

"I have no idea what their record is."

"Even though I posted the lineup across all social platforms for today's game, I don't remember who's starting."

Baseball lingo would fly left and right in conversation and I'd have absolutely no clue what it meant. Many people would get defensive because it turns out I didn't fit into their assumption. Rather than me getting uncomfortable, I'd let them know they're making an assumption about me, showing I'm comfortable in the role, regardless of my interests.

"You understand because of the love you have for baseball."

"*Actually*, I don't. I don't understand and I don't have a love for baseball."

Then, their discomfort instantly shows, which often leads to a response where they attempt to make me feel uncomfortable.

"Wow, I'm surprised you got the job."

"So you're taking a position from someone else?"

"Does your boss know that?"

"Wait what? Then why are you working here?"

awkward uncontrollable laughing

80% of the people who surrounded me while working in sports majored in something completely different from sports. Biology, Communication, Hospitality, Journalism.

I spent day after day after day after day interjecting with questions in conversations, asking people to explain what something means or make a point I didn't know what's going on.

Asking didn't annoy me and I wasn't mad about it. It was just such an interesting situation where I learned how we as human beings assume people know certain things based on many external/internal factors, especially "adults."

Pay more attention to how *adults* act.

When you're growing up as a child, we build the perception that when you're an adult, you'll have your shit *together*. However, once you become an adult, you realize many adults don't embody the "adult" traits or skills you thought they would. You want to talk about managing expectations? It's this. Manage your expectations of adults, AKA people who are simply older than you. 99% of the time, your expectations of adults will not align with your reality.

There's a sizable gap between *kids* and *adults*, where kids view adults as some type of superhero.

We're all just people. No one has *everything* figured out. We're all figuring out our own version of unlearning and learning what works for us.

School taught us to see and view perfect adults in textbooks, yet there are a lot of factors which interfere with that. Some people never "grow up."

You think "adults are adults" but they're still like teenagers with the same behaviors and tendencies.

What does growing up even mean?

Why do people that need to grow up tell other people to grow up?

Why is "grow up" an insult?

What even is an adult?

Am I an adult? Are you an adult?

I still get ID'd when I'm out to dinner, so...

Some things are not obvious to some people, yet some people lead or end a sentence with the word obviously. I've gotten into the habit of saying "what about that makes it obvious?" Or "That's not obvious. I didn't know that."

I get death stares back like "WTF Danielle?" But seriously, it wasn't obvious to me.

Part of my job working in MiLB was to manage the mascots. When I started, this was the process when someone wanted to request a mascot appearance: They'd have to download a PDF, print it, hand write on it, upload it to their computer, then email it to me directly. My expectation: I will receive forms completely filled out with all information needed: location, the day, the address, the actual event, their contact information.

After I review a form, I'll print the form, type up all event details in an email, confirm a mascot can attend, then let the person who sent the request know.

However, that wasn't *always* the case, and honestly rarely ever happened.

I received the form half filled out, then needed to reach out via email to the person who sent the request and ask for answers to the questions they skipped over. Then, I'd have to wait for their response, which meant keeping the task on my to-do list.

The way I see it, though, receiving a half-filled form is not the other person's fault. The lack of follow through on the request is my fault for not setting a clear expectation to include all event details before submitting.

So, to solve the ongoing time-wasting issue, I created a Google form with all questions accompanied by a little star next to each, indicating what's required to be submitted to ensure each mascot appearance form I received would be fully filled out.

See what I'm saying about managing expectations of other people? *Really*, it's managing expectations of yourself and what you're putting out first. See what you can adjust on your end before blaming somebody else. You were the one getting mad about the lack of fulfillment, not them, so what do you have to do to change the circumstances to make it easier on both ends?

This was the same for game days. On game days, I would get frustrated with myself for not having enough great photos of people and fans during the game. I would ask interns to help by being in places I couldn't so I could oversee the promotions, but their follow through never really seemed to work out. Rather than continuing to feel annoyed game after game, I would take matters into my own hands instead of relying on outsourcing as a solution.

There are so many situations where I'd go out of my way to ask someone if I could take their picture to post to our social media accounts. *I loved asking.*

"I know I watch you do this for probably 40 to 50 games now, but I still don't get how you can go up to random people and take their picture," a coworker said to me after I took an adorable photo of twins eating ice cream at the ballpark.

Often I'd go in the middle of a large crowd and yell, "On the count of three, wave and smile!"

These photo ops ended up becoming one of the most fun moments during a game—pulling myself out of feeling like I was doing a job with multiple tasks to accomplish, and into a state of doing what I love.

Then I'd hear, "Danielle, how are you so brave? I could never do that."

See, but you could do the same thing if doing it meant achieving something you knew you needed to do for yourself in order to fulfill your end goal.

I honestly never thought twice about taking photos so openly; it was just *always* something I viewed as intuitively needing to do, never really over-thought about who else would or wouldn't do the same. It put me in an interesting position to think about how things that are so easy or come naturally to some people are so hard and unimaginable to others.

To me, it was as simple as posting content on social media to fully represent the MiLB team experience during a game day. It's about knowing people will judge you, have all the thoughts of negative self-doubt on themselves, then project their insecurities onto you. Yet, you post anyway—Because you see the value, the importance and the impact. It's about exceeding the expectations for brand management and highlighting the brand you're representing in the best way possible.

We start our day by setting an alarm the night before for an arbitrary time. We want to wake up when it goes off, but *fuck*, if we don't wake up, or hit snooze, or set a later alarm, there's a negative thought attached to that. Yet, when there's no expectation of when you'll wake up, your morning will go great, negative-thought free.

"I'll just try again tomorrow," we say to ourselves under our breath when a minor inconvenience happens and we convince ourselves our day is destroyed.

If you can't manage your expectations for yourself, it's extremely hard to manage your expectations of other people.

"Ya know, my generation can't do this stuff. Yours is quick."

"I don't need anyone to know what I'm doing."

"I'm not quick enough."

"I don't have what they're looking for."

"They want someone more skilled than me."

"I'm too young."

"I'm too old to understand this," says the client who asks me to do something social media related to them, as if I'm *good at it because I'm just young.*

You're "too old" or you're just too lazy or uncomfortable to ask questions, learn something new out of your comfort zone, understand it, and figure it out, so instead, you make excuses and expect someone else to spend their time on it for you? Mmmmm.

I used to think this to myself and doubt this is a response that I wanted to be said out loud. But now, I say it out loud.

I'm not impressed by the excuse. It's not helping either of us or allowing us to be better. I've built the credibility, brand, and clientele, where they *literally* come to me to hear responses like this. They know they're working with me to be called out on their bullshit and not allow their excuses to remain their reality. Instead, I teach them to notice their doubt and redirect it.

LEAN INTO DELUSION – 117

For some, it's shocking, for others, it's exactly what they need, but never realized it (I) existed until now.

It's similar to the "OooOoMmmMgGgG, I love TikTok" people, content creators or consumers and the "Yeah, I would never download TikTok," people.

Are you a creator (making and sharing content) or are you a consumer (just scrolling, taking *everything* in)? Or maybe a mix of both?

Do you think someone *actually* doesn't want to download TikTok, or since they've said they'll never download the app for so long now, they feel like they can't go back because the perception of their peers is that they hate it? If they suddenly change their mind and want to go on, they're controversial? They say "there's too much to keep up with" or "I just can't do that," and instead of *actually* believing the things they're saying, they're purposefully putting other people down because they are not strong enough or confident enough to post on their own... even though they *actually* want to.

Whatever your narrative becomes is also what you're projecting your expectation of yourself to be. Half of the time it's an excuse to not want to try something.

I mean, that's literally why my business exists.

If you recognize the importance of needing to be on social media as a professional or a business, but talk yourself out of the reasons you don't want to participate or can't commit, that's what I'm here for.

Your reality is yours, so if you're doubting it, guess what? You're controlling it. Evaluate what you value more. What's *actually* stopping you? Are you making excuses for yourself, or do you not value something as much as you say you do? When there are options to make shifts in your life, are you facing the hard decision and executing or avoiding?

My friend Ty recently interviewed for a project management position he was super excited about. A day later, when he was reflecting on how the interview went, he called to tell me about it.

"D, at the end of the interview, the interviewer said, 'Oh, I guess I have some questions I'm supposed to ask you, but it's fine.'" Ty and the interviewer were so present in the conversation about who they were as people and the experiences they've had, they forgot they were both in an interview and barely discussed the position. They both let the conversation flow instead of sticking to the planned script.

When something is logic and ego driven, you have this, "I don't wanna say the wrong thing" mentality, while also losing the *humanness*. By leading with your intuition, you default to authenticity.

"You can talk yourself into it *or* out of it. Thinking logically doesn't always do shit," a client once said to me.

Regardless of the outcome, Ty left the interview feeling at peace with how it went, how he portrayed himself, and the impression he made.

That's all we can really ask for, right?

Several adults in my life have told me, "Never take a pay cut," or as Prime and Lil Wayne say in the song Hot Boy, "Quick to cut a bitch but never take a pay cut," except awkward, because I *have* taken a pay cut. And I would take a pay cut over and over and over again if this meant hanging on to the valuable experience I had.

In the moment, I decided I didn't want to let money or fear stop me from doing things I wanted to say yes to.

Also, let's agree that salary range or hourly pay needs to be on job descriptions simply because they need to be. We deserve to know what we're about to receive or negotiate for if, after we spend our time to commit to "getting the job," we get the job.

Have you ever gone for a job you thought was a perfect fit for you, then within the interview process were shocked by the hourly wage/salary? Maybe they offered you the job, and you said yes because you worked your ass off for the opportunity? Then a few months went by, the excitement wore off and all you felt was extremely underpaid? Or maybe you turned down the offer because even after all of that effort to prove you were the right candidate for that job, that salary or hourly wage just wasn't enough for you to simply live the lifestyle you were currently living or wanted to live?

Everyone takes an opportunity for different reasons.

I flipped my perfect 9-5 job, for one with nearly unlimited hours in commitment, "giving up my weekends," and basically learning a brand new language I never wanted to learn. I *chose to* commit to that lifestyle. I knew what I was signing up for. I said yes because how could I walk away or turn down a company that said, "We've followed your work on your social media pages, where your work ethic, personality, and drive shine through, and we think this job opportunity would be a perfect match to help grow our brand and yours."

You can't.

I mean, you can, but then at that point, what more are you really hoping for in your career?

Maybe you're one of the many people who wondered why I would take a job in an industry that seemed to make no sense for me.

I've heard it all.

"Wow, what a waste of a weekend," says the friend, scrolling on social media all day or waiting for a guy to text them back.

"What about happy hours?" says the family member who has never been to a happy hour since their college days.

"You're giving up a weekend to work?" says the past co-worker who works late night during the week to get ahead on work just to constantly complain how behind they are.

"Sacrificing a weekend for what?" says the old college friend, who is still stuck in their old ways, using memories & good vibes as a measure of their current success.

People have different mindsets for what the purpose of a "weekend" or a "break from reality" means. Working while others are "playing" doesn't make work any less fun or ~work-like~ if you're doing what you want to do.

"What are your plans for the weekend?" Shane, a close coworker of mine, asked me.

"I'm attending an event to speak about the importance of sharing your experiences in the moment on social," I replied happily.

"Wow, good for you! I don't have the time for that, and I don't get paid enough. You know you don't *have* to do that, right?"

I just stared blankly; *I don't value your opinion, anyway; I prefer my lifestyle over yours. I don't care if I'm not getting paid;* I thought. *I love speaking and sharing my life with other people. I have time to do what makes me happy and can help other people.*

It's the same thing as when you *hate* how someone dresses; you shouldn't take advice from them about how *you should* dress.

Like if they tell you, "I really don't like those shoes with that shirt," then you look at them and you're like; *Well, I would never wear what you're wearing soooo your opinion holds little weight;* You're reminded not everyone is going to align with what you want for yourself.

Conversations like this are common.

I have consistently said yes whenever I'm asked to speak at an event or for an organization. I've driven an hour for an unpaid speaking appearance on my day off that I had planned to spend with my mom. Instead, I brought my mom with me. She watched, listened, and took photos. It was great. Some of the best experiences of my life have been speaking at appearances where they did not pay me.

Whether I'm speaking to a large group of college students at the University of Connecticut (UConn), coaches of the Connecticut Junior Soccer Association (CJSA) preparing for their upcoming season or in a conversation one-on-one, I've *always* wanted to amplify my messages. Now, I'm seeing the return on the time I invested speaking for free. I never did it for a *future reward*. I spoke for free because I was obsessed with sharing my message in hope to inspire others, but today I get paid for sharing the message I love so much.

When I'm under pressure to answer a question or talk about something that I haven't had time to prepare for, I don't try to avoid answering. I say whatever comes to mind; nerves or embarrassment aren't stopping me for shit. By saying what comes to mind, I'm forcing myself to really understand what I think and how I feel about different topics. It doesn't feel like work or overwhelming; it feels authentic and natural, specific to the direct audience.

The reason I love talking out loud is that you're forced to answer in the moment. You have no choice but to say whatever comes to mind—no notecards or essays and definitely no time to take a day or two to respond. In that moment, it's you versus whatever topic you're facing head on. Nowhere to hide. You don't have time to over prepare, overthink or worry about perfecting the sentence or paragraph.

Eventually, when you're put in these situations enough, you no longer want to rely on a PowerPoint or need days to think on something because you trust that whatever you're going to say is what you and the audience need in that moment.

Reflect on expectations you have of yourself; even the ones you don't realize are subconsciously holding you back. It will be life changing. Check yourself *before* you check others.

No one knows your internal expectations unless you tell them. When you have expectations for someone else and they don't know what your expectations are, it's *pretty much* illegal to get mad at them.

For those who went to college, we walk into work environments with our college hats on. We've just recently taken our ethics class, COMM 100 and BUS 101. We know all the terms, the definitions, what we're supposed to do, what not to do, how to act, and how not to act.

Before we know it, we walk into a new work environment and say, "What the ffffffuuuuuuuhhhhhck is *actually* going on? This is all wrong."

You compare *everything* against what you learned. At that point, you can barely focus on your actual job because you're focused on all the other things, leaving you with a *?????* expression on your face.

You know what I'm talking about, the situations where the person at the front desk isn't there on time so rather than opening the door since your hands are full with all work things, you need to now dig into the bottom of the purse to find keys to then unlock the door, hoping your coffee doesn't spill. First world problems, yes, but again, that's a part of their job. Or the person who hides somewhere within the office building to take breaks and read randomly in the middle of the day, yet never meets deadlines but gets mad when called on for their lateness. Or when someone doesn't show up for a meeting, so you hold off on starting, call them to see why they're over five minutes late and their response is "Oh, I never had that in my calendar" or "Oh, sorry I have another meeting I'll hop in when I can."

Your expectations of them are not aligning with what you learned in school, but also with what you would do. You get awkward in your own skin doing what you think is right. The crazy thing? Each of us has cringe stories about situations in the workplace that are just *???*

I mean, I spent months—MONTHS—working next to someone where the entire office said they needed to go—like needs to get fired asap.

"Oh my gosh, he's asleep again at his desk. Do you hear him snoring?"

"Is he for real? Another call with the admin regarding college information for his kids in the middle of the office?"

"Did you hear how he asked Tara out to dinner? How inappropriate."

My expectation of upper management, on hearing these concerns, was that they would address them rather than talk about him behind his back and let the behavior carry on.

What *actually* happened?

Nothing.

Well, nothing *until* inappropriate comments were made directly to my 20-year-old intern, and I was more than outraged. It took little 22-year-old me to be like, "Hi. Um... I know this has been going on for years, but this is stopping immediately. This is toxic and dangerous AF to the victims and the company. I'm not letting this go."

Workplace scenarios like this commonly happen worldwide, distracting you so much from doing the actual job you're being paid for (and most likely underpaid for at that). The additional side of long-term trauma and harassment is just a free unwanted bonus.

This is what's not talked about at all in college. *Nothing.* Nothing about how your expectations of adults doesn't seem to fit the expectation you created during your four (+) years of college (or eighteen years prior). People older than you tell you to ask for help, but they don't *always* teach you to problem solve for yourself when the people you relied on for help let you down.

Realize what you need, do your research and note-taking to justify what you need to be better at your job, for yourself and for the company, and then *just ask*.

I originally wasn't on the planning and executing team for the Yard Goats event the Alzheimer's Association was hosting. But since it wasn't going as effectively as planned, my CEO asked me to join the team to complete the final tasks to move forward. Sometimes the fall through of an expectation works out in your favor.

We're able to connect more now than ever because we have the privilege of social media—the more opportunities we have for connection, the more we seem to be isolated. Even though we know how *good connection* makes us feel?

In an icebreaker at a meeting I was in with the Hartford Yard Goats staff, we had to share something nice about the person to our right out loud to the entire staff. When it was my turn, I was excited. I had to say something I love about someone commonly referred to as *Eyeore* in the office—often negative, low energy, not the most visibly happy guy.

"I love how he says good morning to me, even though I know he really doesn't want to acknowledge my presence. I stare him down when I notice him walking past my desk, smile hard at him, and wait for him to say *good morning*. It gives us a good little laugh to start out the day. It's wild what a small *good morning* and acknowledging someone's presence can do to your mood."

The staff laughed like, *did she really just say that?*

But it was true. His small action, even though a little forced, made me feel welcome. Many other people in the office would walk past one another, or literally be sitting directly across from someone and not say *good morning*.

What the actual fuck is that about?! The lack of humanness was giving robot vibes, and it's honestly a bummer that this is even a conversation.

Sometimes you need to change yourself to accept someone else's possible hurt.

What's the reason someone would see someone else and purposely not acknowledge their presence?; I thought to myself when I'd witness it happen day after day.

I believe if I'm going to work best with someone, it'll happen. If I'm not, someone else will be a better match. Seeing someone else as competition *only* hurts you from understanding who and what is truly meant to be for you.

My clients work with me for my skills, but also because of who I am as a person—who they've discovered I am through conversation. I know my perceived competition, but I'm not discouraged by them; I'm inspired by them. Rather than imitating what they're doing, I often do the opposite. *Intuition check*—that comes from being me, and it's a fact: no one else can be me.

Just like no one can be you.

After I launched Chylinski Media, several people reached out to me about company merch. I decided to look into getting a couple of items created. I was so excited and made it a priority over the last five months of 2020. My branded pink and black crewneck sweatshirts arrived. When my boyfriend noticed the giant boxes, the first thing he said to me was, "Okay, when are we doing a photoshoot?"

Wait, really? We were minutes from walking out of the house to go out for the night, but I smiled and said, "Right now."

"Let's do it," he replied.

I did not expect that response. *But he did.* My boyfriend took photos of me in both colors of the sweatshirt as I posed around our apartment. It was so much fun.

When posting them on my website and sharing across social media, I priced the sweatshirt at $35. This *wouldn't* give me much profit, but *would* share my excitement about my brand. I wanted to share Chylinski Media, my message, and existence wherever I could.

Within minutes, two of my *best friends* messaged me, saying, "Oh my gosh, I want one."

"Send me the size and color you want!" I replied, so excited.

Messages kept coming in, and it was amazing having others express the same emotion as me: pure joy. I collected payments as people reached out, but I hadn't heard from my two friends.

A week passed, and I followed up. "I'm sending out the first batch in the mail today. Venmo me if you want in! I have your size and color saved."

They sent me uncomfortable excuses, blindsiding me when I had been expecting supportive best friends.

Rude? Dramatic? I don't know but it didn't feel good.

"Ugh, I don't have any money right now. Follow up next week!"

The following week, after I'd seen posts of them out at the bar with friends, I followed up again. The responses:

"Ugh, my goal is to pay off my credit card ASAP. Let me know when you're mailing out the next batch!"

"I'm working on paying off some of my student loans right now. Maybe the next shipment?"

I stopped responding.

If they weren't willing to *support* me at such a momentous time in my professional life, what was *I* doing?

The problem wasn't my friends. The problem was me. I had this expectation of how they would react in that situation, and instead, they did the opposite. My expectation of them didn't match what I would have done for one of my best friends. However, I can't expect someone to meet me halfway *ever* when I recognize we're all on different journeys of healing, self-love, and out-ward facing love.

If someone wants to follow up with you, or follow through on a commitment they made, *they will*.

I'm a big believer that not *every* friend you make is meant to be in your life forever. Each person serves their own purpose in your story, and sometimes their chapter gets cut shorter than you originally hoped.

Anyone who is worth your time *in real time* will not *make* you chase them. When someone gives you a piece of information based on their actions, you're now in control of choosing what you do with it next.

13. Doubt Happens

Someone once told me extroverts continue to make introverts more introverted, even if they don't necessarily want to be. Extroverts hate the awkward silence, so they continue to ramble when it seems like the other person has nothing to say. When in reality the introvert is waiting for the extrovert to stop talking for a second so they can contribute to the conversation.

Introvert: *I'm so awkward, no one's bringing me into the conversation. But if I try to speak up, I'll feel like I'm interrupting. Okay, it seems like this thought is coming to an end. Once they finish, I'll hop in. Fuck, someone else just started talking next. I'm never going to get in a word. Will they think I'm quiet? Rude? Ugh.*

If you're someone who finds yourself interrupting people, recognize there are people who would never interrupt someone, who would rather stay silent and never share their thoughts or ideas.

Extrovert: *Okay, if I just talk fast, I'll get my point across and it'll be great. I may be over telling this story, but it's fine. It's a great one. They need to hear it. I can't wait to hear their response. Okay, wait, they're not really responding. I guess I'll tell another quick story so they have some more context. Maybe too much context, but it's fine.*

Subconsciously, conversations carry so much doubt.

I think about this at least once a week; the importance of recognizing the power in allowing an "awkward" silence to happen, hoping other people will step up and speak.

Imagine if you never shared about a *single experience* with anybody. Where would you be? Think about something that you wish you had told more people. Where do you think you would be now? Would you still be at the same job? Would you still surround yourself with the same people?

Guess how many people have told me they don't update their LinkedIn profile (or post anywhere across social media) when they get a new job because they aren't sure it's going to last? Hundreds.

They'd tell me things like:

"I want to make sure I feel comfortable and confident in my role within the company before I really make a public announcement."

"What if I hate the job and quit?"

"What if I post and my future coworkers think I'm already bragging?"

"I don't want people to know my *every* move."

When you're hesitating or doubting whether you *should* proudly share experiences that light you up, I want you to remember that it will *only* bring more opportunity that aligns with you, not less.

You may inspire someone else while sharing what you've gone through and how you ended up where you are. You are opening the door to conversations that could change the trajectory of your life and those around you. The more comfortable you are with sharing and celebrating, the less you allow doubt to stop you.

Imagine if I allowed the negative thoughts about not being qualified enough or not having a background in sports to cloud my desire to celebrate and share this milestone in my career? The potential outcome of sharing was greater than my fear of posting.

I was quick to open up about not having a sports background and not doing a lot of research beforehand. It felt easier to be open about my reality upfront, rather than for people to think I knew it all. It seemed like a lot of effort to pretend to be someone I wasn't. By trusting the people who trusted me enough to give me the opportunity, I didn't hesitate to post because I was excited—excited to share about a new chapter in my life that I never thought would be offered to me.

Sharing doesn't *equal* bragging.

Have you caught yourself diminishing the achievement you were about to share by putting a negative statement before it? Or maybe you've never noticed, but you're thinking about it now because I'm calling you out LOL.

The beauty of recognizing negativity is that you can distance yourself from it. By never repeating specific moments of negativity, and never over-thinking, then the direct piece of negativity that happened for a few seconds will never need to be relived. The moment *basically doesn't exist.*

Just share the achievement. *Just* accept the excitement. *Just* embrace the success.

There is no need to say:

"I don't mean to brag, but..."

"I don't usually brag, but..."

"I know this is going to sound like I'm bragging, but..."

"Ready for this humble brag?"

You are allowed to thrive parallel to others without the constant thought of comparison or competition.

There are two types of people. You have the, "If you don't brag for yourself, who will?" And then you have the, "Share your experiences as much and as often as you can, because you never know how it'll connect you to new opportunities."

When I left the Alzheimer's Association for the job with the Hartford Yard Goats, for example, I shared as much as I had the capacity to.

I posted to LinkedIn, Instagram, and Facebook hoping my network could help me make sense of it all: "January 2nd, 2019: I let my New Year's resolution choose me this year. I thought spending more time with baby goats & coffee was a FABULOUS idea. I am so so excited to share that I have accepted a position at Dunkin Donuts Park with the Hartford Yard Goats as Marketing & Promotions Manager." Attached was a photo of me sitting in front of the stadium.

Guess how many people this post reached on LinkedIn?

Over 300,000 people in three days. Most of the public comments were from people I've never directly interacted with before.

"Awesome! Congratulations! Wishing you much continued success."

"Hi Danielle... Sounds great.. You must be very excited. Good luck on your new venture!"

"Congratulations Danielle! I know you will be great in this role and they're lucky to have you!"

"Great work. Hope 2019 is your best year ever!"

Seeing the power of social media and the impact I was already having in a position I hadn't even started yet was interesting. The support from some people I've never even met compared to people I've known for years differed.

"Is this a joke?"

"Girl, it's not April Fool's Day. What's happening?"

"Wait what? Huh? How?"

How could the people who know me the deepest doubt my abilities and decision making to take this new job?

This is why I love social media and LinkedIn, specifically. You see the support, you see people sharing their happiness in your happiness and feel what they're *actually* saying to you: "Hey, I see you. I see what you're up to. Keep going."

14. You vs. You

"I've been so excited to do Real Estate, but after a few months, I was tired of it. I'm not loving it anymore. I don't know what to do," a woman shared in an Instagram video.

"Why does there have to be such a strong reason? Why can't it just be that you no longer want to do it?" a man responded.

"Could it be burnout? Like, do you think I'm just overworking myself?"

"Why are you so dramatic? Why have we trained ourselves to think we have to be burned out to no longer love something? The answer is clear: you just no longer like what you're doing; you liked it yesterday and now you don't like it today as much as you did. Your passion changed, so your direction will. *It's okay. That's life. That's being a human.* Now come to terms with yourself and be comfortable making other people uncomfortable, which is walking away from something you've spent time on where people are expecting you to continue doing."

No one is stopping the woman from walking away from her current job or industry and into a new one. The doubt that comes from what other people think about you is what can make you panic in the present, making you feel unsure, like you have to keep going and *push through,* even though you know your heart is no longer in it.

Just walk away from it.

It's that simple, *in theory.*

It's a never-ending cycle. *Learn, unlearn, learn, unlearn, repeat.*

Our society is structured to build workers, not thinkers; *They* don't want us to think or reflect *too hard.*

"This is how we did it last year, so this is how we're doing it again this year." Sound familiar? I think we've all heard this phrase in the workplace at some point.

We're like machines at work, instead of human beings pausing and spending enough time to strategically evolve.

When I was at my first job, my mom, a woman who has worked at the same company since she graduated college, told me more than once, "Never leave this company, Danielle. They have great benefits. Keep contributing to your 401K."

I listened to her advice until I received another job offer that allowed me to walk into work as *Danielle*, be *Danielle* all day, and leave work as *Danielle*—working with like-minded high-energy millennials, maintaining an extremely active lifestyle, constantly moving and interacting with hundreds of people daily all while in a brand new baseball stadium.

Did walking away from a job that I thought I'd be in for longer make me a quitter? *No.*

Did my decision to make a leap into a new industry open myself up to other professionals judging me and thinking I'm unqualified? *Yes.*

Would I let someone else tell me what to value more than feeling great and doing something that would make me happy? *Hell no.*

The goal of life isn't to figure it out or check off a box; the goal is to follow your intuition and do what feels good to *you*.

I'm constantly creating, changing, and determining what success means to me daily. What success means to me today might not be what it meant to me a year ago or ten years ago, or in one year or in ten years. I am allowed to change my mind and celebrate those changes—and you are, too.

Unlearning the things you thought were true can be uncomfortable. It can make you feel like you're doing something wrong, like taking a mental health day when you need to. Burnout doesn't happen when you're doing a job you feel *yourself* in. It happens when you're pushing through a situation or experience that doesn't feel good *over and over and over* again—ignoring your intuition. The real burnout is living for other people and their beliefs rather than your own.

Living for the weekend is not ideal, yet how many people do it?

Many experience such an unhealthy work environment that they grow to think *this is how work is supposed to be*, because that's all they know. The same goes for relationships, too.

Transitioning from working for someone to working for myself, I learned how I've *never really* worked at 9-5. I've always worked a 24/7/365—walls down, boundaries pretty non-existent and only in *sport mode.* The beginning months of Chylinski Media looked like me rolling out of bed, walking a few feet to my office and opening my laptop. The sun would rise and set, and my butt wouldn't move from my chair except when my boyfriend would remind me to pee (not kidding). Even worse, I'd only eat or drink when he'd bring me a snack or re-fill my water.

I always *joke* saying my business is only successful because of him, mainly because he literally kept me alive. That, and he also introduced me to a lawyer so I could set up my LLC immediately, instead of continuing to push it off. A man who supports me like that? Count me in.

Our worth is not measured by our job title and productivity level. Yet, it's ingrained so hard subconsciously in our brain. What job you hold, how long you hold it, and what people think is a successful job or career does not have to be how you define success.

A client of mine named Timmy, a kind-hearted man with a landscaping business, asked, "Would you be mad if I had someone on my team take over the socials?"

I was managing the organization's social media accounts for months, posting for them regularly and engaging. Timmy wrote the first check to Chylinski Media.

Timmy had reached a place where he understood what his organization needed in terms of social media. He experienced the impact social media had on his company, what types of posts work and how they translated into business. Timmy believed someone on his own team could now use those similar skills to relay the organization's authentic message daily on their platforms.

So how did I react? Did I go into meltdown city because my first client ever told me he no longer needed my help and was choosing to walk away from me?

"Oh my gosh, no," I said. "Not at all. That is literally my goal. I'm here to act as a resource when you feel you don't know what to do next to be and feel successful, but when you do, you let me know. If you have someone internally on your team who you feel could handle and take over what I'm doing for you, that is the ideal situation. I *only* know so much from afar. Having someone day in and day out who understands your processes, workload, and vibe is what will show 100% authentically who your company is."

Timmy thought success *to me* meant getting and keeping as many clients as I possibly could. But in reality, my mission is to help clients feel as confident in their online presence as they can. They deserve to be happy and fully aligned with how they come across online and be able to fully represent their own brand. That's what Timmy could now do, which is why I see him as my first successful client.

Have you been in a situation where someone made you rethink your idea of success?

If my idea of success was to get as many clients as possible, I would have felt bummed. But I had helped Timmy grow by putting a social media process in place that he could slowly replicate and shift to his own team.

This was a day of success for me. *Me*, an actual business owner. A girl who makes her own money, on her own time, for herself—in total control.

We all have different ideas of success and rely on different things to help us become successful.

In college, my planner allowed me to feel like I was maintaining success. I would write which week of the semester we were in along the top so I could fully keep track of how much time had passed, what I had already accomplished, and what I still had to do before the semester ended. Doing so allowed me to stay on point and on top of time.

My friends knew me as the girl who *always* walked around with her planner and wrote down *every* single thing I could, so I wouldn't forget.

Friends wanted to get lunch? *Added to my planner*. Meetings for the clubs and other organizations that I was involved in? *Added to my planner*. Parties planned for the weekend? *Added to my planner*.

I would look at my planner before bed, and then the next morning before leaving my dorm room. When I was completely aware of what was in my planner, all aspects of my life could run smoothly.

Feeling natural over feeling comfortable in a situation felt better for me once I understood the difference.

Taking my backpack off, putting it on the ground in front of me, unzipping it, pulling out my planner, flipping through to the correct week, checking if I was free for lunch was uncomfortable as fuck, yet still felt natural. By denying wanting to grab my planner, I'd be denying who I truly was as a whole person.

Being natural means being confident in yourself and not comparing, but rather embracing *you*.

When I graduated, there was the world of digital calendars that I felt thrown into. For a little while, I no longer saw the need for my paper planner because I could do all my planning online—*one less thing to carry,* I thought. But eventually I was reminded I thrive off my paper planner. My planner is exactly what keeps me *me*. I thrive off of the ability to write things down—appointments, deadlines, ideas; you name it, it's written in there—in one place. A place that I wouldn't lose or accidentally throw away. Something *only* I could control and check off once completed.

My planner looked like a hot mess to someone who isn't me, but allowing myself to commit to it looking that way helps me live my life as *me*. It's not chaos that *gets in the way*; It's chaos that's *real*. It's chaos that feels *natural to me*.

People around me have said, "Why do you even use a paper planner now if you can do it all digitally? *So delusional.* You could just have it on your phone and never have to carry it so you'll never forget it."

I remind myself—*I know and am aware of what does and doesn't work for me and my reality.*

As you and I continue to evolve into the best versions of ourselves, we need to find what works for *us*. There's a balancing act between putting ourselves first, while also recognizing the impact we have on others in the process.

"The best thing I learned is you don't have to respond to everybody," Ana, a well-respected and successful woman in her industry, shared with me over a drink at the bar. Such a simple message, but something that has stuck with me.

If you want to answer, answer. If you don't, don't. Listen to what your intuition is telling you and run with that rather than a set of guidelines some other business owner or TikTok video is telling you. You decide what's right and wrong for you. No one else does.

It's easy to find yourself in *take-take-take* relationships rather than mutually beneficial ones. I don't endorse running yourself into the ground for people who aren't as committed to you as you are to them—but sometimes in the moment; you don't know that's what's happening. Break for people who wouldn't even bend for you? Don't.

Just because *everyone else* is doing or saying something doesn't mean it's best for you. Did you just get triggered to a flashback of a parent saying to you in 5th grade, "If **insert your best friend's name** jumped off a cliff, would you jump too?"

We often catch ourselves saying *cute trendy sayings* like "the struggle is real." And if you're super committed, you're even buying a t-shirt with the phrase on it.

As a society, we need to stop justifying things with clichés and start taking accountability. For example, saying, "Time is flying by," when in reality, we are doing our best to be in the moment and remain present. Or how we joke, "Guess what my screen time was last week?"... but it's not funny, yet we all *joke* because the number is astronomically high each time, almost mind blowing. When we take a step back and process the literal words coming out of our mouths, it's terrifying what we're unconsciously projecting onto ourselves.

The struggle was *actually real* when drama went down in middle school.

You had to spend the entire night overthinking by yourself in your bedroom unless you really felt the confidence to pick up your house phone and call a friend's house number, hoping they picked up rather than their parents. You know, because we couldn't talk to one more person who we weren't planning on; that sounds hard and scary... and not worth it.

Or when we couldn't do our homework because we forgot our book at school and you'd call *every* person in your class you could find in the phonebook, and still no one answered or had the book or they just lied and didn't want to give it to you.

They *wanted you* to struggle. They *wanted you* to perceive yourself as a failure so they would feel better about themselves. That's when the struggle was REAL—the lack of ability to communicate effectively and timely.

Isn't it funny how we used to be terrified to make a call to a friend, and now we're facing similar pressure, but with higher stakes?

When it's *You* vs. *You,* what's stopping or distracting you from prioritizing yourself?

Confidence Check

As a human, you have a constant need to feel significant but also a fear of being seen. Conformity is easy because it's comfortable and there's *minimum* risk. Lack of confidence comes from trying to be something you're innately not. Understand the responsibility you have in life to express and embrace confidence to thrive as an individual.

15. Don't Chase, Attract

"Fake it 'til you make it" has been a phrase used by management teams in various jobs I've had. The phrase in my top 2 least favorite phrases in the world, along with *living the dream*. When I first heard it, I was confused and kind of shocked. I often embraced the moments I was in and opportunities I had, even when they didn't *always* feel the best.

But fake something?

Could never be me.

I heard people using the phrase followed by an eye roll, or a laugh, or intending to imply... *Is this day over? We're almost done. 1 more day. 4 more hours.*

My reality?

I never wanted the moment or the day to end.

I chose not to embrace this *fake it 'til you make it* mentality, even though all staff members around me were. If anything, when I heard it, it made me *fake less* to where I realized I had *already made it*. So many people were faking positive emotions externally, while feeling negative emotions internally.

I would fake nothing.

I mentally didn't know how.

Instead of suppressing how I was feeling in those situations, I would have a conversation in order to find a solution that allowed me to be present. Maybe it's rescheduling a call, taking an *actual* lunch break, taking a day off to do nothing, learning ways to calm my mind, drinking water or learning how to confidently ask more questions.

LEAN INTO DELUSION – 141

Choosing to stay in a toxic environment instead of either removing yourself from the situation or addressing the cause of the negativity adds up. I'm not saying you *should* be or will feel 100% *every* day. However, there are healthier ways to work through the *off* or *down* days instead of telling yourself *fake it 'til you make it.*

Work can be mentally exhausting, even thinking about walking into the office or just getting ready to go, nevermind how exhausting doing the actual work may be. This is especially true if you are surrounded by or interact regularly with people who do not respect you the way you feel you *should* be respected, or the way you expect them to.

"Is this a paid or unpaid high school summer gig for you?" a father asked me as I stood next to the dugout waiting to bring his kid on the field for an on-field promotion at the Hartford Yard Goats.

How do you respond to that besides wanting to say, "Who the fuck do you think you are? I'm clearly 5'10ish, I'm clearly older than 21. This is obviously either a full-time or part-time job."

Is this question funny? No.

Demeaning? Yes.

The management when I was an Orientation Group Leader in college constantly used "fake it 'til you make it."

A few weeks prior to starting, we received a giant list of around 180 questions, varying from when the school was built to the hours of the dining hall. First, we were expected to find the answers. Think of this as a giant scavenger hunt, except instead of searching for Easter eggs, we were learning as much information as we could about the University. Once we found the answers, we had to memorize each of them so we could share the correct information in conversation with incoming students and their parents over the next two months.

Inevitably, questions often arose, "What if we don't remember the answer? What happens when we're so exhausted from running on a few hours of sleep that we can't even think straight?"

The response was *always* some form of "fake it 'til you make it." *Fake it 'til you make it, but also be 100% correct in the process.*

It made me crazy. I would fake nothing. If I was tired, it showed. We weren't superhuman. If I was unsure of something, I'd find someone who could provide the correct answer. If I didn't agree with someone, you knew. When we had to leave our final reviews, I filled the entire response with why *fake it 'til you make it* is toxic:

When someone doesn't know what they're doing, they also use *fake it 'til you make it.* They tell themselves to keep pushing through and eventually they'll have it all figured out. *Eventually,* they'll be comfortable. *Eventually,* they'll be confident. Regardless, they're not *actually* faking anything. The people who say *fake it 'til you make it* are probably the same people who say *living the dream.* It gives openly fake and sarcastic vibes. Even though it's a mindless response, they're putting out some not-so-good energy into the world, for themselves and for others.

You have the ability to bring conscious awareness to what you're doing and how you're acting. Living the *fake it 'til you make it* mindset works to undermine your self-confidence by creating a belief that you are not up to the task at hand, but have to pretend that you are.

This doesn't mean that you have to have all the answers 24/7. It just means to be true to yourself. Be as confident in what you *don't* know as you are with what you *do* know.

There are people who don't think about how these little enhancements to their work days can leave a long-term impact on them.

I feel so fortunate to experience working in environments (both of my past two full-time jobs, prior to self-employment, and now) where I share about my job regularly while reflecting often.

I've spoken to hundreds, maybe thousands, of people, classes and groups at this point. I've received many comments from coworkers or other working adults:

"You're so brave for going to speak."

"How do you do that? I could never."

"What a waste of time."

"You're not getting paid for that, you know."

"How do you balance that and your work?"

"I'd never drive over 10 minutes for something like that."

I've had some of the best experiences of my life speaking at appearances I *wasn't paid for*.

Despite all the comments from coworkers and other working adults discouraging me from doing unpaid speaking appearances, I did them anyway because it felt authentic and natural. I enjoy being under pressure to answer a question or talk about something without having time to think about it rather than having it due at a later date, and I've learned to say what first comes to mind. When you have to talk immediately, you're forced to dig deep, understand what you think and how you feel about many aspects of your life.

When you're coming from a place of happiness within, and wanting experiences to fuel that, *you just get it*. When you're living a life of "not in my job description" and "I don't get paid enough to do that," you don't.

It's not healthy to let people's perceptions of what you do, how you do it, or what it looks like take over your mind. Acting as *you* will attract the right people.

It can be challenging when people around you can't tangibly see the ROI of having genuine, random conversations with others. It's because you're living in *different* realities. Some things you're just meant to attract. It's why Coffee Date with D exists, so we can have solid conversations that remind us of the importance of trusting our intuition and talking on the spot—the messy, raw version.

Something typically seen as "not-put together" or "less-than-perfect" or "something to feel guilty about"—like a messy bun—has become the brand of my business. For me, it's both professional and *on brand*.

When the pandemic hit, we suddenly left Skype in the dust and Zoom became a *way of life*. I'd roll out of bed two minutes before a Zoom call, hopping on with my messy bun.

"Aw, look at you being on brand."

LOL, on brand or just sleepy and lazy? Same thing at this point. Thanks for noticing.

I've allowed a messy bun to become my confidence. At first, I'd be like, *Is this too messy? What if they don't want to work with me because I look like this? I should have started getting ready 30 minutes earlier to straighten my hair. Ugh.*

Something society has made us, as women, feel guilty, unprofessional and messy about, now has a whole new meaning. I redefined the messy bun to give it a new meaning. Now if you ever get backlash for a messy bun, just *blame me.*

I mean *thank me*, LOL.

Anything we can do to make us feel more comfortable in our day to day, one less insecurity, we should do it.

Now, when I'm tired of my hair getting in the way, I don't hesitate to throw it in a messy bun and get back to being productive.

Let's normalize chaos because no one seems to talk about it enough.

Integrating the idea of being true to yourself, even in places where the temptation to be fake is strong, will be that one step forward you need to live a completely different life.

Implementing the philosophy *pics or it didn't happen* into my daily life throughout college and into the workplace have never meant document *every* little detail or share *everything* you experience. We're not designed to pump out content 24/7/365 for people to consume or share their opinions in the form of comments. It didn't take a cliche to make me realize the behavior behind it directly correlates with brand awareness, but the phrase helped me justify the importance of documenting, personally and professionally.

If you're putting a lot of effort into something but not posting about it on social media, you're missing out on invaluable brand exposure.

The more you share things that make you *you* and light you up, the more you will connect with like-minded people—the exact people you're seeking, consciously or subconsciously. Give people who don't know you as many opportunities as possible to find you, recognize you, and acknowledge you. Those who are meant to relate and be attracted will be.

Bottom line: Post for yourself.

I encourage people to post wherever, however and whenever they want. My thoughts on posting—you're posting for when people land on your page, whether they heard about you, searched you, or randomly landed there, rather than for immediate gratification or validation that may (or may not!) come in the moments right after posting.

You never know how your posts can encourage someone to reach out to you or which post will push someone to make the leap and connect.

I shared a post on LinkedIn during my first year in business that read, "100 INVOICES!!!!! Last night marked 100 invoices sent for Chylinski Media! Between 1:1 strategy calls, monthly social plans, to long-term contracts, brand revamps, new websites launched & logos created. We've landed here together! In 2020, we learned. In 2021, we will execute accordingly. Stay committed to your decisions, but flexible in your approach."

Shortly after, I received a LinkedIn message: "I was thinking about how I need to find someone to help my company with social. I logged onto LinkedIn, the first thing I saw on my feed was your post saying how you hit 100 invoices, and I thought; *Wow meant to be*; and I reached out right away."

That's how quickly it can happen *for you*.

Let your people find you. This can apply to you as a business owner, employee, or simply existing in your day-to-day life. The easier you can make it for people to find you, the better. Use social media as you see fit personally in your life, but not to a point where you feel anxious. Each platform's impact is different.

One of the most frustrating requests people reach out to me with is: "Make me go viral." When someone focuses on trying to go viral, they're no longer posting for themselves or sharing who they *authentically* are. Sure, going viral can feel great and maybe overwhelming. Often people are so focused on the outcome that they're not aware of or in tune with the process, or, more importantly, the personal progress that comes *through* the process. They care more about seeing their work shine for a minute rather than feeling the vibe or conversation between them.

My LinkedIn post about joining the Hartford Yard Goats felt great to share, yet going viral was never the reason for sharing my career update. Instead, this post was a perfect example of the power of LinkedIn and the reach you *could* achieve by showing up as yourself. Building a personal brand online requires consistency and going viral once or twice is a short-term win on the journey of a long-term goal.

Another tough request I get as a business owner is when someone asks me to send them a social media portfolio or links to accounts that I've worked on so they can look. I get frustrated and often flustered. Each client has different guidelines and goals for social media, which makes it difficult to curate an aesthetically on-point portfolio. Some clients are working with limited budgets and minimal existing content. Other organizations might have a bigger budget, but bigger limitations on what can be posted. In either case, a perfectly planned Instagram grid is not the outcome. I cater to each client's varying and specific needs. We as human beings are not one-size-fits-all.

People who want to be chased are not for me. I don't *need* clients who embody "professionalism," who look like they "have it all respectfully together," who fit the mold of the businessperson coming out of the College of Business. I want the *chaotic* person who is searching for ways to be themselves at all times, no matter the environment.

What is making each of us think some things are so easy or that some things are so hard? The simple answer is limiting beliefs impact the way we see our life.

It's the same thing as when I go to my aunt's for Easter and I'm the oldest cousin. It *always* turns into some type of photoshoot—*not complaining*. LOL. The 2 boys, my brother and my younger cousin in middle school, are the ones that are begged or forced to join. The other 4 girls span high school through college and are here for the sorority pics. Then there I am, the 5'10"ish girl right in the middle standing normally, like "hi." Compared to my younger cousins, I'm *old* and *outdated*.

I mean, you're talking to a girl who started college at a time when our dorms didn't have Wi-Fi. We had to use ethernet cables (if you're reading this and you're like WTF is an ethernet cable... we've clearly had different struggles and I'm sad about it. Go Google it.) to use our laptops.

I'm that age, but still also so young... But, the deeper answer is that we are straight up in our own way, letting our fears outweigh our potential happiness.

.

16. External Reflects Internal

While on vacation in Florida, my family planned a day of swimming with the dolphins. They planned a photo op later in the day, so naturally, my mom and I did all that we could to keep our hair dry so it would look good for the picture. *Good.*

Once I got the picture back, I didn't even like how the picture looked. *Did I seriously spend the whole day not getting my hair wet just for this trash photo outcome? Damn Danielle.*

So here I was thinking about how I wasted my day so I'd look *good* in this picture swimming with the dolphins... even though the natural thing to do when swimming with dolphins would be to have wet hair. Who was I trying to impress?

This same insecurity resurfaced whenever a friend invited me to pool parties in high school, or even to their house for a swim—immediate panic. You would not catch me going underwater. Underwater meant flat hair, runny mascara, black eyes, ugly dried hair, and maybe even weirdly dyed hair. When I'd spend so much money dying my hair, or when I used to spend an hour curling and straightening it when I was getting ready to go out, there was no way in hell I would sacrifice that investment.

I missed out on a ton of fun things because I cared too much about things that didn't matter—like wet, chlorinated hair. Why *should* I care if my hair is wet and flat?

Looking back, I want to tell myself, "You're dumb. Get in the water."

In high school, I had a friend who didn't own any sweatpants or sweatshirts. You wouldn't catch her dead wearing them. She wouldn't go to sleepovers because she didn't want to be seen in *lounge* clothes.

These types of vibes are so self-limiting.

Present yourself on the outside in a way that reflects how you think of yourself on the inside.

Donate or sell things in your closet that don't make you feel you. Too pilly? Tag hurts you? Sweating through? Bra straps keep showing? Hurts your feet? Too tight? Too loose? Brings up bad memories? A gift you never wanted? Get rid of it.

This goes for your physical appearance, and also for your social media content. All these pieces of your external appearance can align with who you know you are.

Choose to be comfortable, which shows up in many forms—clothes, hair, sneakers, jewelry. Your look, your stance, your posture, your words. You don't have to be or look or say one thing.

People have interviewed me, and I've interviewed countless others. I've seen them say and do things to prove themselves that did *not* feel authentic.

I never wanted to be that. I don't want to be that; I'd often think to myself.

Have you ever thought about the energy you have when you're fully you? When you are in love with what's going on in the current moment, are you aware of your energy? How would you describe it? What does it feel like?

If you embrace your highest potential, rather than being embarrassed about not fully aligning with others, you will not care about the outside noise. Yes, sometimes it's important to be aware of your appearance and the fact that your *every* move is being judged. While this shouldn't change who you are, it will affect how you feel. Embrace who you are, and confidence will follow.

When we adapt to our environment and learn to feel comfortable with the uncomfortable, we are able to experience more of life on our terms. The alternative is to allow situations to dictate how we feel, which *only* limits the experiences we have.

After four months of running around and sweating it out in pants during *every* baseball game I worked at, thinking—*be pretty and confident, but also struggle so hard to maintain that. Smile consistently, but also push through the immense amount of sweat...Got it*—I finally bought a skort (a skirt with shorts beneath it)—size large and extra large, even though I'm usually a medium.

If I go a bigger size, it won't be as tight-fitting or reveal as much of my upper legs; I thought. This outfit wasn't being chosen based on appearance though; I wanted the ability to move around freely at work, still appear professional and do my job without having to worry about feeling constricted or showing sweat through my clothes.

I walked into the bathroom with another coworker and brought both of my new skorts with me. She had worked in the industry for years so I valued her opinion.

"Okay, I'm going to try on both sizes," I told Teagan. "You tell me which one looks better. If you think they both look *too tight, too short*, or *unprofessional* at all, let me know."

Teagan gave me a look that implied, "Okay, here we go."

We both knew that no one else in the office had worn a skort to a game before, so we weren't sure *what would happen*. But we also didn't have any women in upper management to ask for advice, so...

I ended up going with the size large skort, making me feel confident, professional, and comfortable, while still allowing me to do my job successfully.

I'm going to keep the tags on in case it is a problem, and I'm not able to wear it again, I thought to myself before walking out of the bathroom and back into the office.

After a few minutes of wearing the skort, my boss walked over.

Knowing I had *broken* the dress code of khakis, my brain was like *Fuck. Fuck. Fuck. Fuck.*

"Dani, I like the tennis skirt."

Sweet. Approved. Fuck yeah, I thought to myself.

My boss' approval was my *only* concern, since he was overseeing and evaluating my job performance. No one else's opinion mattered or had any influence, so I thought.

A few months passed. The team *only* had a couple of homestands left in the season. HR emailed an updated dress code policy to the entire staff, including photos of *what to wear* and *what not to wear*.

Guess what was in the not-to-wear section? *My skort.*

Well, skorts in general, but since I was the *only* one in the Front Office who had ever worn one, including my intern following my lead, *my skort*. We were then called into HR and asked to not wear skorts again.

How was my decision to wear an outfit that made me feel confident, professional and most comfortable doing my job successfully against the policy? Or maybe, *why* is an upper management staff of all men creating a policy for how women *should* dress in the workplace?

When my intern and I asked about the reason for the immediate switch, HR told us there was your typical old guy, gray-haired season ticket holder who said *employees' outfits were inappropriately short, and it needed to be addressed immediately.*

Hmmm... Are we just gonna ignore the fact that an old man commenting on young women's appearances is also inappropriate? The same guy who complained probably thought that women shouldn't have even been working there or been in the industry at all in the first place.

It can be mentally exhausting thinking about walking into an office and simple existing, never mind how exhausting doing the work itself may be.

Working in sports, especially MiLB, I had to learn to love all angles of myself. *The put-together me* in the office and in meetings. *The sweaty me* running around the ballpark and the sweaty me from pure anxiety trying to keep the show on track. *The messy me* during and after pulling the tarp on and off the field.

I remained confident in all those roles, though, because I had no other option but to be. If I wasn't, then I was doing it *for them*, not *for me.* I'm here to play the part *they* hired me to fill, but I'm also here to *still be myself.*

I regret worrying so much about getting my hair wet growing up, but I sure as hell don't regret wearing a skort to the ballpark.

What does your mood look like when you walk into work? What are you wearing? Are you excited about your coworkers seeing your outfit that makes you feel confident? Or are you worried your outfit isn't *enough*, or it's *too much*? Are you blasting music in your car on your way in or are you so anxious that you don't even realize the car is silent?

Wow, all of that is... a lot. These questions are important to ask yourself, though, before stepping inside the office building where you're going to spend more than half of your waking day (unless you fall asleep at work, hey... I've seen it happen).

Sometimes the perception of how to act while at work can become harder than the work itself.

Through conversation, one of my clients mentioned to me how he hates wearing jeans.

"Wait, what? *Every* time I've met with you, you've been wearing jeans."

We'd been meeting for almost a year.

"I know I know. I just don't know what else to wear and I'm afraid to wear pants that are different than the norm."

Okay, we're buying this dude new pants ASAP; I thought to myself.

Whether or not he realizes, showing up daily to talk about his business in jeans is doing him an immediate disservice before we even start talking. Showing up in a way where you don't feel yourself or comfortable in your skin (clothes included), you're automatically affecting your confidence, and how you choose to speak about yourself.

The low key identity crisis personally creates an even larger one for you professionally. This is especially true if you are surrounded by or interact regularly with people who do not respect you, or want to support you in being the best version of yourself.

Let's make you look as good online as you do in person, and the same for your business, or the business you work for. *That's my goal. Always.*

Building a personal brand is not about creating a character that people will want to buy into. It's about focusing on who you are in the moment as a person, how you want to share more of that with the world, and how you can set expectations for yourself that allow you to show up for yourself—unapologetically—*every single day.*

A close business friend, Lyla, someone I had never met in person until recently, helped me decide on my business brand colors. I needed my brand colors to look as good as I felt about them. I wanted them to fully represent me, aligning words with colors that embodied who I am as a person and as a business.

We began by talking through what makes me *me*—my hobbies, habits, tendencies, go-tos, and more.

"I love chips, and eating chips for breakfast. No shame," I told her. "I also get super pale during the winter. So pale where people ask, 'Are you sick? Do you have a cold? Should I call 911?'"

"Alright, let's start with the varying shades of pink," Lyla said. "Since you mentioned chips, I thought about salt, which made my brain go to Himalayan salt, which is also pink. What do you think?"

"Oh, love it! I have a Himalayan salt rock on the corner of my desk. You can't see it on Zoom, but it's there. Also, chips with a tint of pink are a dream come true. Sign me up!"

"Sweet. One down, onto the next! This next one reminds me of Moscato wine, and the lighter shade could be 'pretty in pink'. Thoughts on those two?"

"Did we just become best friends? My go-to wine is pink Moscato. Yes! Eh about the pretty in pink, though. Let's come back to that name and go to the blues."

"Sounds good," Lyla agreed.

Next, I suggested, "Let's Google some nail polish color names because they're usually fun, quirky, and will give us some good on-brand inspiration."

"Here's a random question. Do you like Disney or Disney movies? This light blue reminds me of Elsa. Let It Go... Olaf... Frozen...?"

"No, but I had a friend, Emilie, who worked at Disney, but literally hated her life and told me that if anyone asks how she's doing, tell them she's loving life. Anyway, I mean, I'm constantly cold aka frozen. My hands and feet are kinda numb as we speak. LOL."

"Hahahaha okay, let's lock it in. This second shade of blue has me stumped. We might need to go to Pinterest for inspiration, so I'm skipping it for now and moving to this white-ish color." She smiled, half kidding. "What about winter tan?"

I burst out laughing. "Maybe winter tan is my new comeback when people ask me if I'm sick because I'm so pale. YES. I love it."

After an hour of scrolling Google, exploring Pinterest, and sharing words, phrases, and sayings that crossed our minds, we finalized the list of brand colors for Chylinski Media. I needed my brand color names to not *only* feel good, but sound good when using them in conversation, while also looking as good on the outside as it feels to me, on the inside. Rather than trying to tackle this experience by myself, I found someone I trusted who had my best interest in mind.

The best part?

This became another fun core memory for me.

The way you act publicly is up to you, which becomes your personal brand, but thinking through an exercise like this will help you better understand who you are so you can better serve yourself and those around you.

Whether or not you have a business, *you are a brand*.

The sooner you're aware of your brand guidelines (tone of voice, values, colors, how you show up, what you entertain, the whole vibe), the more in-tune with yourself you can be. And when locking in your guidelines, be picky with who you let in, filtering *everything* through your own personal lens, allowing your vision to become your reality.

17. Take Back Your Power

When I was on the track team in high school, I couldn't *even* bench press the 45-pound bar. My arms were skinny and would hyperextend. My all-male coaching staff told me to *just sit to the side* and wait until the next part of the workout. I was never confident in my physical strength because the people I hoped would believe in me didn't—so I struggled to believe in myself.

After college, I decided to start CrossFit instead of going back to the hometown gym (my comfort zone). The idea of starting CrossFit was terrifying. Ever since I had knee surgery in 2010, I made *every* excuse in the book to avoid certain movements—CrossFit required all of them.

Walking into the gym *every* day was the goal. Whatever happened inside was a bonus.

The excitement *wasn't* real.

Each time I walked in, I was like *WTF am I doing here?*

The first week, most of my PRs (personal records) were 35 pounds (legit just the bar), with the primary goal of simply carrying my laundry basket up and down the stairs without getting tired and out of breath. I know I was paying for unlimited classes, but *holy fuck*. Someone telling me what to do. How to do it. When to do it. How heavy to do it. A nightmare... yet, I knew I needed it.

It was extremely awkward to be in a class with other people and have a coach inches away from me, watching my *every* move. What a bizarre feeling—receiving instructions on the workout to then have multiple questions on *wtf did the coach just say*, to then finding the confidence to ask for clarity to then complete the damn workout.

Push press, just the bar. I can do this, I thought to myself.

"10 minutes on the clock. Go ahead and start!" the coach said out loud.

My version of start wasn't exactly what I thought it was going to be. I got under the bar, ready to lift, and nothing happened.

Stuck.

No movement.

It wouldn't budge.

The 35 pound bar was *too heavy for me.*

Fuck. How am I going to tell her I literally can't lift the bar? Oh my god. Sweating, not from lifting, but from the fear and anxiety that was brewing up inside of me.

"You can start now," the coach said to me directly, walking closer to my direction, after noticing I still hadn't moved for a few minutes.

"Oh. No, um, I've been trying. I just *actually* like *literally* can't."

She and a guy next to her started laughing uncontrollably. "What do you mean? We don't say *I can't* in this gym!"

"Like I *literally* can't lift it. It's too heavy." I started laughing too, *so hard* that my eyes were teary—but teary because I was about to bawl my eyes out and was trying to cover it up.

I realized then the *only* comparison I could make in the gym was to myself—to the person I was yesterday, a week ago, a month ago. It was *me* versus *me*. I began to set goals in the gym and *cheer for myself* when I'd hit them.

A month later, "OMG, a new PR!" I'd share with my coach.

"Awesome! That looked way too easy, though. Go heavier, add 10 more pounds"

"The fuck? I can't fucking do that," followed by a hard eye roll.

"Just try to and watch what happens," my coach would say back.

Each day held a new challenge in learning my body and knowing when to push myself. I started doing lunges, squats, and box jumps. I got tricked into doing a rope climb. I learned double-unders, handstand push-ups, and so many other things I never thought I'd even try, let alone successfully accomplish.

In order to believe I was capable, I used to think I needed someone to believe in me. I slowly learned I needed no one else to believe in me besides myself. I saw my own strength, *finally.*

Three CrossFit Opens later, I felt less intimidated by the people around me and solely focused on surviving the competition. I maxed out most of my lifts way past 100 pounds, with a solid increase from when I started. I became so focused on myself, what I could control, and the power I had to own the situation. All other distractions became background noise.

Looking back, this was the #DontWasteMyTime mentality in its purest form. Chicken nuggets didn't matter. My self-deprecation didn't matter. All that mattered was the respect I showed myself by taking on the challenge of CrossFit.

You can blame your past and stay stagnant for so many reasons, or you can understand what's most important to you and take control of your life.

By telling myself *I want to commit to exercising so I can successfully carry my laundry basket down the stairs;* the goal became much more achievable for me. When something makes you uncomfortable, figure out how to reframe (AKA trick yourself) so you can continue forward. Sometimes reframing isn't necessary, but taking back your power always is.

I barely told anyone I was going to CrossFit six days a week for almost a year.

"*You would* do CrossFit," they say in a condescending voice as they looked at me—a skinny, solid 145 pounds, long dark straight hair, 5'10ish woman.

This is exactly why I didn't tell anyone sooner; I'd think to myself every time that was the response.

When I finally realized I was confident in my skin in and out of the CrossFit gym and the impact it had on my life, I created a social media post about it to document my one-year milestone. I was terrified.

But, as with most leap-of-faith posts, what happened once I shared was incredible.

This post by no means had the most engagement in terms of likes or comments (public instant gratification).

Likes and comments have nothing to do with *you* and *everything* to do with *them*. You can't rely on someone to publicly go out of their way and say something positive.

I'm going to let you in on a secret about backend engagement details. Backend engagement, *only* what you can see in the settings, includes all the non-public stuff: when people click for more, click on your profile to learn more about who you are, click on the link in your bio, share the post with someone, or save it for later. Backend engagement allows the person engaging to be less vulnerable and can be more powerful than likes and comments for the one receiving.

Guess how many people engaged with the post? 5,130.

Profile visits? 710.

Likes? 363

Comments? 26.

We're in this world where instant gratification is what we usually value and talk about most, mainly because it's whatever anyone on the outside can see—"Did you see how many likes my picture got?"

However, I know many people don't leave a like or comment, or support something meaningful to them, for fear of revealing "too much" about themselves. Some people are more willing to ask questions privately because it can be easier to be vulnerable and more open when the entire world isn't watching, judging, or critiquing.

For this post, the two largest numbers are backend numbers—numbers that the average person would never see unless I chose to show them; the reach was 5,130 people and profile visits were 710. On the outside, it *looks like only* 300 people support me and 26 people felt the need to cheer me on.

Externally, it doesn't look like many people are as supportive of my CrossFit journey as the ratio of the reach shows. If I chose to focus on the external validation, I would be bummed. Or, I can pay attention to the way people *actually* were interested, which was clear on the back-end. I love nerding out at the way people choose to be, or not to be, on social.

Your happiness is not dependent on the number of likes or followers you get on social media.

People have their own stuff going on. You *can't* expect them to support you when they can't support themselves.

How often do you comment on other people's stuff?

Think about it this way. How many times do you see a billboard, then a radio ad, then a tv ad, then a social post, then hear someone mention the company, then see another billboard until you reach out to the company? The same goes for your social media posts. Each interaction you make is one more touchpoint; you cannot predict if someone will need 1 or 100 before *or if* they ever choose to interact with you.

We don't care about likes... or the iced coffee you think you need. We care about reach and backend impressions. We can talk about the direct impact you're making by your experiences reaching others—and whatever they take from it is not *always* your business. Many often look for immediate gratification to justify their happiness. We need to be focused on long-term impact, but that doesn't seem to be valued much any more.

From the outside, people notice how you act, what you look like and choose to wear, and how you respond to situations. They aren't afraid to provide unsolicited input, either.

My mom had been this person to me. Based on her upbringing, when she saw me looking *messy*, my mom couldn't help but say, "You can't go out in public looking like that," or, "Danielle, stop slouching. Stand up straight. You have long legs for a reason. Use them!"

In elementary school, whenever we had to line up by height, no girls surrounded me, *only* boys, because I was *always* the tallest girl and taller than most boys. Growing up, I slouched in group photos—I bent one or both knees. I hunched my shoulders forward, trying as hard as I could to distort my body. I'd nearly hyperextend my knees to be shorter like *everyone else*. I did anything I could to *fit in*.

Then, twenty-four-year-old me was sitting in on the National An-them auditions for the Hartford Yard Goats with my boss, Cameron. A tall high school girl in heels walked in to audition.

Am I gonna cry right now?; I thought to myself as I started to choke up.

The confidence she showed by coming out not *only* to sing, but how she confidently wore heels at her age, was admirable. I saw myself in her so much. She owned exactly who she was and embraced being tall.

I want to be her when I grow up.

I *only* wore heels a few times growing up, one being to my Senior Prom in high school. I spent more than $400 on my dress after search-ing for weeks and going to dozens of stores. I loved my dress; light blue, rhinestones and bling all along the top half of the strapless dress, with a high low cut on the bottom. The dress filled me with confidence, fully aligned with who I felt I was in that moment—put together, *yet* messy, *but* fun *and* bold.

My date was my high school boyfriend. We were standing alongside fifteen+ other couples, getting ready to take a group photo. In front of all our friends and their parents, he yelled at me, "Why would you wear heels?"

Oh...

That was maybe the last day I purposely slouched in my entire life.

My boyfriend tried to embarrass me because he was insecure in his own skin and didn't want to be shorter than me.

Rather than slouching more for him, I stood up taller for me.

Learning to find inspiration while allowing your intuition to guide you will keep you grounded. Reminding yourself of your worth is challenging when you fall in a slump and look for external validation.

I was so used to working to pay off my loans until they were gone. *Every* waking second I was thinking about those loans hanging over my head.

The idea of *owing someone anything* was not what I wanted to be a part of.

I wanted to feel free.

So I made sacrifices to get those paid off. I couldn't mentally afford to blame the fucked up system for them. *Giving away* my money held more worth than overwhelming my mental space. And, now I'm in this position where I have money. Not *money* like I'm going on vacation *every* month *money*. But the type of money where you realize things you thought were so expensive are so far out of reach growing up, really aren't.

There are some things I bought over the last 10 years... things my parents didn't understand why I spent my money on them, mainly because it wasn't a part of their ideology—too far out of reach for *them* in *their* reality.

Mine was different, and they didn't realize yet.

I learned to create my own beliefs, and I learned to unlearn other people's views of *expensive* or ways to spend money.

What's something growing up you thought was extremely expensive, so far out of your reach until you were old enough to be for it on your own? What's something you're continuing to work through and unlearn?

"I want to lead," Demi, another MiLB team employee, shared with me on a call. She had reached out looking for career advice. "How do I gain that trust level where I don't feel like I'm being micromanaged? I want to prove that I can be a good mentor. I know I lack confidence, but it's hard to build when I don't feel supported at work. I'm not sure if I belong here, but I want to be here."

Kind of heart-breaking, right? Hearing her say these things out loud was a lot to take in. Demi recognized she wanted to change her reality and was looking for help to do so.

I'd ask questions back, "But why? Why do you want to lead? If you want to lead, lead. Your ego can easily get in the way. Humble yourself. I recognize taking the action is harder than saying you want to do it."

Even months after, nothing seemed to change—still complaining. She wanted help, but Demi created no change besides telling herself, "I can't, but I want and need someone else to tell me how and why I am capable."

She's looking for a walking self-help book. She asked the wrong girl.

Each time I speak with people, I hope I'm mirroring their truth back to them in a way that allows them to see it more clearly.

I'll call you out on your bullshit that you may or may not have noticed before—I will mirror you, reflecting back to you what you're already feeling.

Asking for help is hard. Like, *really* hard. This is *everyone's* first time doing this thing, ya know, being a human, living life and acting like they know what they're doing. You are so significantly different from the person next to you. By keeping your vibration up so high, you can not *only* be yourself, but you can be happy in what you're saying and how you're presenting yourself non-verbally.

18. Expressing & Recognizing You

I received a DM from a LinkedIn connection, Logan: "Hi Danielle! Your personal branding and marketing has done you well! And to think you've done it all with *only* one photo, too! My friend Owen noticed we're connected and asked me about you. I was like, I don't really know her, but she seems to kick butt. I'm sure Owen will reach out as I suggested! Hope you are well!"

The photo Logan referenced was my profile picture across all social media platforms at the time. The picture was from one of the *few* times I left the house later in 2020 for a *foodie influencer dinner.*

Before eating the main course, another attendee, Jill, asked me to take her picture. I said *yes* because I love to do that shit.

Once I got all the angles on her iPhone, I hesitated, but then blurted out, "Do you mind getting one of me, too?"

It surprised me to see how I looked, completely different from the vibe I had before quarantine began. The current version of me: hair messy half up half down, drink in hand, wearing a new outfit I threw together minutes before running out of the house.

A few days later, I updated my profile photo, the one Jill took of me. By no means was this your *traditional* headshot (yes, I cropped out the drink in my hand), let alone a planned and curated photoshoot.

I was me.

Does your profile picture look like you—the real *you*? If I've only seen your profile photo and was meeting you for coffee, would I be able to find you in the café?

I didn't realize the moment I updated my profile picture; I was rebranding myself and my network was watching closely. That's something I couldn't have planned.

Life is meant to be lived, not planned. Nothing a business plan could have predicted or made happen. The wildest part? I almost didn't go to the event. I almost backed out at the last minute.

"I just don't feel *me* enough to go right now."

"You're going," my boyfriend said. "You're *always* you."

Why is he always right, fuck.

Small decisions can make way for big opportunities when you're yourself.

Build a brand and a social media presence that embodies and aligns naturally with you, not one you need to keep up with.

"Build character instead of *a character*," a client told me.

Exactly.

Authenticity and living a life you love, take pride in, and can share naturally is the goal.

We've been conditioned to try to be robotically perfect, yet when someone *is*, it doesn't mean they're confident. The confidence you see in other people is not linear. Confidence is a journey within itself. However, we often see confident people as *always* being confident. Some days ya got it, other days you're like; *Holy shit, what is going on, girl?*

Recognize who you are, who you're around, and what the environment is like when you're confident. Just like with happiness, the same goes for confidence—they are not destinations, they are choices. Your reality is a place where you make the rules, and being confident can be one of them.

"You've had the journey I envy," someone recently said to me.

You DO NOT know my entire journey, I thought, yet they truly almost did based on how much I share about my life online.

Someone else mentioned, "All of your posts are so happy and I love them. But what about when you're really sad? Where are the posts about those?"

I laughed. I rarely go on my phone when I'm sad. The last thing I want to do when I'm sad is go on social media, nevermind post an update, "Hiiiiiiiii, I'm sad. BRB. TTYL"

"I think that's something to be shared," she said back.

I was questioning myself. "Am I not posting enough content about *sadness*?" I literally can *only* make content when I don't have time to make content or I hit a point of delusion LOL. My *sad* posts or thoughts are rarely expressed in the moment, yet the feelings and lessons are expressed through posts to follow.

Before social media existed as a way to express such wide gratitude, real, tangible, paper cards did.

I used to write friends in middle school cards for holidays; Christmas cards with candy canes taped to the envelope and Valentine's Day with a Hershey kiss or two attached. You name a holiday; I was making cards for it. I would hand write cards with in-depth personalized messages for each person, *literally hundreds* of cards. I remember sitting at my parents' kitchen table, exhausted, wanting to give up, but I had so much love to give and I would not let my sleepy eyes stop me. My mind was stronger than my body's desire to fall asleep. I was confident I would find the power to stay awake.

The next day, I would pack up the cards and candy in my crocheted Abercrombie, Limited Too, Hollister and PINK tote bags. The cards would get sorted by class and time of day, so I knew exactly where each person was when.

The next morning, I'd get on the bus with four giant tote bags in my skinny, fragile arms filled with love letters, expressing my appreciation of friendship. I'd start with my main peeps on the bus, and would just continue handing them out throughout the day.

Little me, not knowing what a GPA was or letting anything other than myself define my confidence.

Recognizing confidence in places you don't realize you'll have it, in theory, will give you more confidence. Being aware that when you *look and show up* the same on paper, online and in real life, existing becomes that much easier.

I used to go to my Student Senate advisor's office for meetings in college, and I'd just randomly start crying.

"Why are you crying right now? What?" She'd stare at me, confused.

"I don't even know. It's just hard."

Am I really a college student bawling my eyes out to a grown woman? The fuck am I doing? I'm so annoyed. This is so embarrassing.

Sometimes, you have all of this confidence where you don't even realize is confidence, and once it hits you, it can be extremely overwhelming.

She'd remind me, "You're crying because you care."

When you accept yourself, you're no longer self-sabotaging or trying to harm others.

When I first started working for the Hartford Yard Goats, I would often go to my boss with questions around posting and managing the team's social media accounts. I'd get up from my desk, walk like 20 steps to Cameron's office down the hall, and ask one of my go-to questions— "Does attaching a link in this tweet make sense? What media companies *should* I tag in this announcement? Is this #BREAKING hashtag at the front of this post necessary for this? How does this look? *Should* I edit anything or just hit send?"

Cameron would look at me and pause. "Danielle, this sounds like a question for the Social Media Manager."

Which was me. I was the Social Media Manager.

I would stare back at him. "Ah fuck. You're so right. Got it," and I'd walk back to my desk.

I had to find the courage to swallow my ego, walk into his office, stand face to face, ask a question that was keeping me from moving forward, knowing I was uncomfortable and unsure of my next step. He would remind me I was in control. *I had the answers.* He didn't have the answers for me.

Embrace being uncomfortable because there is *so much room* to grow. Stop overthinking. Stop second guessing and follow your gut.

After plenty of conversations like that, I got to a point where I stopped asking about a lot of things. What I had learned about the organization's mission and goals became second nature, and my decisions then stemmed from intuition.

Eventually, I fully and authentically embodied what the organization represented. There were a lot of new things I was continuing to learn, but I didn't realize I continued to learn how to not doubt myself. I put myself in a situation where doubting wasn't an option because they hired me as the expert.

There is not one person within the company who can do what you do. The "I'm not afraid to sit alone because I know what I bring to the table" quote is no joke.

I've been to a few funerals and my heart would pound for those who would have to go up and speak. I would think to myself, "Oh my gosh, I could never stand up there alone. They are so brave."

Until I did it.

My Dziadek (Grandfather in Polish) passed away in October 2019.

For as long as I can remember, my dad and his dad seemed to know who they were, *always* fearless in being themselves. They would smile, laugh, and dance around together, in a way that made it so contagious that you couldn't help but do it yourself. It seemed like they *only* had one version of themselves—one they weren't able to tone down or dim. They were the people in the room together who would crack jokes, do anything funny for attention and randomly ask if you wanted a shot of vodka during a time that made absolutely no sense to the average person.

Sorry Mom, this is where I'm not average.

Leading up to the funeral, my Dad called me and said, "Danielle, would you be comfortable doing a reading at Dziadek's funeral?"

I didn't think twice. I wasn't afraid. For *everyone* I was afraid for in the past, I now see why they weren't afraid either. *Something* happened to them before they got up on the podium to talk—some experience that allowed them to feel the confidence they could to speak successfully.

After digging in to discover what made me say *yes* so quickly, when I knew the old Danielle would've panicked and said, "Let me get back to you," I finally understood.

I just spent the prior 10 months outside of my comfort zone. *Every single day* I'd get on the microphone at a Hartford Yard Goats game, which had allowed me to say, with the utmost confidence, *yes* to speaking at the funeral.

The idea of somebody passing away in our family was so foreign to my entire extended family. Whenever I'd be in conversations with people and they'd mention how their grandmother or grandfather died, I would give my condolences and try to feel their pain. But honestly, I never felt it. I never understood it. I *always* thought in the back of my head, "That doesn't happen in my family. No one in my family has passed away, and I can't imagine anyone in my family ever passing away. We are all so strong, happy, and healthy."

That's the thing, right? We try to know all that we are, but sometimes we forget the things that we're not. We're not invincible, and things pop up that we would have never imagined—like the pandemic that hit in 2020, leaving so many people jobless.

Somehow, we find a way to push forward. We continue to be this version of ourselves we try to be happiest in. We recognize all the external factors that can get thrown our way when we least expect it, but at the end of the day we *have to be* happy with who we are inside. While misery can happen around us, it is on us to reorient towards happiness.

We're taught all these things to "*not be*," like someone with visible tattoos, a person who swears or has public social media pages—Because if we do those things or are those things, "You'll never get a job." We really straight up let our society tell us what to change about ourselves as individuals solely so we can be accepted and live just to make money.

Guests of my podcast often wait for me to send them questions I plan to ask, or notes on what to prepare for, *even after* I told them I'm not. Eventually, they realize I'm *seriously* not sending them anything other than the calendar invite with a Zoom link.

"No planning Danielle? I know you said no planning but..."

Yeah, I really meant no planning. I was confident when I started Coffee Date with D, in both myself and any guest I would invite on. I meant it when I shared that we literally were on a hypothetical coffee date.

Do you typically show up on coffee dates with a list of questions and start firing them off? *No.*

I find it eye-opening to experience what's shared when you speak from within and allow conversation to unfold naturally and flow. My intention in being a host that does not send questions as prep is that it conveys to you I'm confident you'll show up and say exactly what needs to be heard. I'm giving you permission to recognize that you're much more confident in your natural state than you may have thought.

Get comfortable expressing and recognizing you.

You Decide

Seems *obvious*, right? *It is.* How you choose to represent yourself directly aligns with what you'll attract into your presence. Remain aware of what is and is not working in your decision-making process, putting into perspective what changes you can implement daily.

19. That's A Post

Here's where I'm at: One post, one video, one caption can change a person's life. The longer you wait to post, the more of a disservice you're doing to your community. The longer you play by someone else's rules, the longer you hide behind your shadow, the longer you let your limiting beliefs take over, the longer you let your negative talk win.

Did you know who I was before you picked up this book? *Maybe* you heard about me through word-of-mouth. *Maybe* you follow me on social media. *Maybe* a friend passed the book along to you. *Maybe* you saw the book cover on Amazon and you clicked *add to cart*.

Social media is *real life* and *meant to be* social.

Show up as you are *without* feeling the pressure to be perfect for the approval of others, but to be dipping into many things.

I've been posting for and about myself for as long as I can remember—diary vibes. I show up for my personal brand by continuing to establish, create, and share myself. Rather than *only* moving through experiences, I experience *and document them*. Sure, they are often basic everyday stories, but through sharing and reflecting, the impact they truly have on my life is revealed.

For example, there was a time where I was late to a meeting at Starbucks. Rather than dropping what I was doing to make this meeting, I texted the person I was meeting and said, "Hi, can we meet 30 minutes later? I have this burst of energy and creativity right now, and I want to film a few videos before I head out."

"Sure, no problem at all," he said. "See you at 1:30 at Starbucks."

Once we were sitting together, he said, "That was *really cool* you texted me and asked to push back the meeting."

"It would have been *really uncool* of you if you were in that situation and prioritized me over you, not thinking I'd understand," I said.

Read that again.

In the moment, I *really* wasn't asking him if he minded. I was giving him the chance to feel that the decision was mutual, respecting both of our time. I continued to explain, "I was going to be 30 minutes late regardless of how you responded."

"Wow," he said back. "Wow," as he took a minute to unpack what I had just said.

It's moments like these that I think are important to not *only* share but also to reflect on.

"If I didn't push back the meeting, I wouldn't have been able to show up 100% mentally for you during this hour we scheduled to talk through your business together. That would be unfair to both of us. Ego aside, I needed to text you."

Someone may read that and say; *WTF? Who does this bitch think she is? Did she not just talk all about #DontWasteMyTime?*

In reality, the *wasting my time* part, for me, would have been if this man said, "No, that's not okay with me."

It's not okay with you if I listen to my body and do what I feel is best for it in this moment so I can better serve you? Got it.

I've been working with this client for over a year, and he's finally seeing how the things I've been telling him are what I've already integrated into my life.

He sees himself in me, while all along he's been working with me to *see him in himself*—he just didn't understand that until now.

It's always a great day when my clients have these epiphanies.

When I shared online I started a business, the business came *running*. Why?

"You have the luxury to have connections that genuinely care about you," a new business owner said to me when meeting up for coffee. It makes me think; *Wow, he's right. Yet, all he's seeing is a cute young, energetic extrovert, but dismisses that I've been posting authentically as me for 10+ years. That's something I can't teach. You can't buy my 10+ years of building true connections like you can buy followers.*

"How do I get that? I've been to a ton of networking events and I just feel like it's not working," he said to me, feeling inspired, yet frustrated.

"But if you're *only* doing it to network, are you looking for connections? If you're looking to *only* network, then *good job*. If you're looking for connections, then... *crickets*. But, yeah, that makes sense, it's not working because you're going with the intention of making sure you get *everyone's* business card, judge it before you *actually* put their information into your phone or follow them, and then you're onto the next person. It's all surface level. How do you expect someone to genuinely advocate for you when they don't even know you? They just know that your business card *should've* been made a different color or you *should've* used a different font." I said back to him.

By continuing to share my experiences, I'm reminded of how I didn't take the traditional approach or have a *standard journey* of finding a job, progressing in a company, or switching companies. Through sharing on social media, we can bring attention to how we *actually* live our lives—not how we wish others could perceive us.

There is not one person who has the exact experience that you do.

You bring something different to each moment.

Putting real-life scenarios and feelings online allows other people experiencing similar emotions, or those who have already gotten through them, to resonate and connect with you. This is real networking, unlike when someone writes, "Hi, I'm Bob. I'm looking to expand my network. I hope we can connect."

Personally, resume builder was never in my vocabulary, but I've been in many rooms where it has been for others. When saying "resume builder," people are implying they're doing something to "build their resume," even if they don't care about it or it makes them want to jump off a cliff.

Why do something to make yourself look more appealing on paper to someone else?

You can choose to spend your time on things you want to—things that align with who you are, who you want to serve, and how you want to serve them. You can choose to do things to build your resume, but those resume builders only build an *impressive* sheet of paper if that's your mentality and reality, not necessarily you as an *impressive* person.

Sure, we can track the number of followers or numbers of likes we get, but what does that *actually* mean? The goal *for me* is to have meaningful conversations with people who respect and care about what I'm doing and want to be on this journey of life with me.

What this new business owner is not seeing and has overlooked is the *non-professional* work that led me to this *professional moment* and has shaped the decision making in my life.

"You've been doing so much inner work in your 20s."

"Yeah, because I grew up thinking adults (anyone older than me) would be one way, but then in experiences with them I'm like, *wait*, adults aren't *adults*. The same grown people who told me to dream about a job, husband, and respect are suddenly the same people repeating daily, 'I hate my job. I hate my husband. FML.' All the things they told us we're supposed to love, they actually hate. And not only do they hate, but they spend their time talking about *what, how much, and how often* they hate. Adults want you to learn comprehension skills at a young age, but then when you implement them and call them out on their shit, it's *not cool*. When another adult calls them out on their behavior, they get mad. But, when a kid does something they don't approve of, the adult yells at them and the kid is supposed to be better and learn from it... I'm supposed to respect them but when they don't respect me, I'm supposed to let it slide and stick around?"

He just stared back at me like *holy fuck*.

I continued. "I encourage people to show up as themselves, but they get confused as to who they actually are because they've constantly been told who they *need* to be. I've realized your personal life and how you show up in business are completely aligned. I spent my whole life trusting adults would help me love and craft the life I live, yet they're the ones who taught me their perceived importance of keeping *the two extremes* separate. If what they're telling you to do makes you hate your life, why do you need to do it? You're seeing the results to let someone else talk for you."

Stunned, "So what do I do? How do I get people to have genuine conversations with me to get to know each other?"

This is where we're fucking at in society—a 50+ year old man, asking me, a 27-year-old woman, how to have *genuine* conversations so they can have a *successful* business.

Am I the *only* one saying *what the actual fuck* in my head (and often out loud)?

I'm glad I finally put my ego aside when I did. I often think about how I would have *actually had to look and apply for jobs* if my social media accounts were never so public. The online presence I'm creating can freak some people out. I've been told that I'm so *brave for oversharing*, but a life of *oversharing* has been a life worth living for me.

My college campus was fairly small, with about 2,500 undergraduates. During my freshman year, my approach to social media was this: If we didn't say hello or acknowledge each other when we were walking around campus, I wouldn't accept your follow request or follow you on social media. *The fuck is the point? Let you stalk and judge from the sidelines when you can't make time to give me a wave or say hi in passing?*

If I deleted anything in my past, I wouldn't be where I am today. That's a part of my story. Archive, fine, whatever. But delete? Never. It's okay for your social media pages to reflect where you've been, where you are, and where you're going.

Who are you following?

Who are you letting follow you?

What are you consuming?

Where and how often are you consuming?

What value are you getting from your time spent?

How do you feel when closing out of a social media app?

How do you feel when opening a social media app?

Are you able to change any of your answers to those questions? (The answer is yes.)

There are plenty of people who straight up haaattteee on social media, but we know a lot of positives can come out of it. *Rather than blaming the Mark Zuckerbergs of the world, maybe you should blame yourself?* Just a thought.

Let your opinions *of yourself* drive your thoughts and actions, not the opinions of others (real or imagined). Use your social media accounts to document whatever moments in your life you want to share. This is why finding a niche and only posting content that aligns can be harmful at times, limiting us to share more about what we intuitively want about ourselves for the sake of *saving the aesthetic*. We remain vulnerable in the hope we will find people who align with us and our purpose.

Being vulnerable isn't necessarily about connecting with *them*, it's about being open enough for people to connect with *you*. You provide the space for a genuine connection to be made.

"I feel like I'm talking to my future self right now," I heard on the other side of the zoom call after I responded to an Instagram DM from a student who had reached out to learn more about how I got to where I am today. Comments like these keep you aware of your direct impact on the world.

To those reading who are like, "K cool Danielle, but I'm still not going to post," let's switch your social media perspective.

Why do you want followers? Not paid followers, real followers. How do you want to get them? What do you expect of them? What do you want them to do once they're following? Oh, also, you know followers are *actually* human beings, right?

By sharing experiences & documenting, we're bringing awareness to how we *actually* live our lives. Putting real-life scenarios and feelings online allows other people experiencing similar emotions, or those who got through them, to resonate and connect with us. This is the real networking, not the type of networking where we say some real robot shit.

People are looking for others to fill positions, not just looking for someone with a set of skills. They are looking for someone who has a personality that fits in with the existing team, someone that will bring value to meetings, someone they look forward to grabbing lunch with, someone they can send work-related memes to, someone they won't feel the need to roll their eyes at. This is where you can use your personal brand to your advantage. Your consistent and authentic use of social media will allow someone to gather all the information they need before they spend any of their precious time *or yours* with an interview process.

Think back to a time when you didn't feel confident, yet it's likely someone who crossed paths with you likely viewed you as confident.

Were you *actually* confident in that moment? Eh, maybe not.

Is there *always* an explanation? No.

Is perception of reality different for each of us? Yes.

This was one of the things I noticed when working in MiLB. I was so *go, go, go* I had little time to overthink. On one hand, less overthinking led to little time available for doubting myself. On the other hand, it was a fast track to burnout.

How do you feel in environments where you need to decide quickly?

"How does this work?"

"What packages do you have available?"

It may feel easier to select a standard option instead of talking out your actual goals.

Can you imagine walking into an office and, after sharing your vision, the so-called expert essentially tells you without any fluff, "We're going to make you basic AF so you can blend right in with what *everyone else* is doing. You're going to post what I *tell you* is the best to beat the algorithm."

However, in these situations, *what's the best way I can help?*

When working with another person, *an actual other human being with feelings,* dreams and desires, it is vital to keep an open flow of communication instead of telling them what to do.

Instead of worrying about whether I'm saying all things *perfectly*, I focus on making sure they know all of their options by having an open, free-flowing conversation. We talk through goals, time commitments, budgets, and more to gain a better understanding of their needs.

No one learns and grows by *always* being given the path. Rather, they grow when they learn how to create rules that work for them and forge their *own* path. Staying open to vulnerable conversations will help you play by your rules. Each of us are different and need special adjustments. By laying out multiple options or multiple paths someone can take their business, it opens their mind to new ways of thinking and sparks ideas they might not have had otherwise.

In college, I was the Social Media Manager for my Class Council, although no one used that term yet.

We were doing a countdown to the Senior Formal and honestly; I was lazy in my attempt to create a non-ugly and annoying countdown. My brainstorming was coming up completely blank. Instead of taking on all the work myself, I turned to being *actually social* on social media.

This is the post I sent out: "We're counting down to Senior Formal! There are under 20 days left. If you're interested in being the featured picture for a certain day, DM us! If your number in the countdown gets accepted, please submit your photo so we can post on the according date! The *only* requirement is that your photo needs to show the number of days left until formal."

Students were so excited. People I had never talked to reached out to take a number and thank me for the fun opportunity. I posted one daily.

Sometimes I'd get a DM like, "OMG I'm so sorry. I forgot to take the photo for today."

"Just take it right now!" I'd reply back.

And they would.

The photos ended up being funny and so random because the lack of planning encouraged spontaneity. I low-key was facilitating people into being authentic and trusting their intuition in the moment versus letting them off the hook by skipping out because they forgot to or just didn't follow through on their original plan.

The campus community looked forward to seeing whose picture was next and how they portrayed the countdown for the entire senior class.

Imagine if I *hadn't* sent that tweet out.

Imagine if I *had* waited until I felt like I had a perfect plan in place to take public.

Little did I know, what I was doing then was preparing me for my career. In that moment, I didn't realize my reality could do something similar for a company no matter what the goal was, to enhance their brand, to gain followers, to get donations, and so much more. Going to college to learn is one thing, but recognizing what you learn outside of the classroom is where the real value comes in.

Did I doubt I was going to get a job? *Yes, kind of.*

From that point on, it was up to me to put in the work to find something I aligned with.

"You'll never believe who made it in the paper. It's a photo from the other day when you were hosting the Alzheimer's Awareness night with the Hartford Yard Goats at Dunkin' Donuts Park." My dad held up the paper, waiting for me to respond to him with my guess.

My parents attended the event to support me, and somehow, they managed to make it in front of the camera. "I *actually can* believe it," I laughed.

I cut the photo of them out of the page and hung the clipping on the wall of my cubicle at work, right next to my laptop. It was right in front of my face when I worked at my desk. Six months later, I was working for the Hartford Yard Goats.

When you find yourself in situations with an extreme amount of pressure, you have two options; trust you can push forward and do just that, or give up. By following option 1, trusting yourself forces you into a position where you need to fully trust your authentic self. I never understood these options "existed" or which path I was taking until I spoke up more about my experiences with people close to me.

Growing up, my mom was aware of the Law of Attraction and how to use it to her advantage. She'd play the tapes in the car on the way to soccer practice or when she'd pick us up from a play date. I just remember her *always* happily bouncing off the walls.

"Why don't you have bad days?" I'd ask her. "Why don't you get as mad at things like I do? Why do you get over things so quickly?"

She'd somehow find a way to never let anyone, or thing, ruin her day. What I never understood is how human beings can switch their mindset *whenever* and *as often* as they want.

People, situations, events, etc. are coming into your existence for a reason. Life isn't just "happening to you," it's happening *for you*. The more that you're aware you can control your thoughts to attract the things you want, the more control you'll feel while achieving the results you want. And sometimes, you'll realize what you thought you wanted isn't *actually* what you truly want. Embrace the change and opportunities—after all, you're the one making change happen.

Rather than digging and trying to find the perfect company or the perfect position, I stuck to what I knew and allowed the things I have shared about myself, my skills, my journey, my experiences to do the work for me. My bosses found me because I was building my personal brand without even knowing what I was doing—before it became cool to talk about having a *personal brand*.

Suddenly, I was in a position where I was being asked to do professionally what I had been doing for myself all along.

20. Facts & Feelings

When I started working for the Hartford Yard Goats, I asked my boss, "What's the actual social media strategy? What's the goal?"

"Total world domination," Cameron replied.

I thought to myself; *Okay, I think I can do that, LOL.*

I realized strategies and full-on plans around social media aren't *my* thing.

If you want to be genuine and respond to the present moment by following your intuition, there can't necessarily be a plan.

You'd *always* feel behind.

But when you trust that *present you* knows what's best, the outcome can be incredible. You'll naturally want to post, and lean into that feeling. When you fully embody who you are, or the brand you're working for, the right content will come.

I'm not anti-marketing plan, but I am pro learn who you are as a person and a business before all of your focus on growth and strategy is for a non-breathing thing, like a business.

The acronym ROI gets thrown around like crazy.

Like, what about it? Don't care. Not impressed.

Not *every* action should be centered around an immediate return on your investment, and sometimes you may never be able to measure the return. When it comes to *actually being social*, the return is intangible.

While on a call with another social media manager named Kenzie, she was drilling me with questions about impact measurement: "Danielle, how do you measure ROI for your clients' social media accounts?

No measurable ROI? What's your reach? How can you tell if you're reaching your target audience? Who are you impacting?"

"Not every post has something that can be measurable. If you're so caught up on what's measurable, then you miss the point of social media. My clients have to trust the process."

The point of social media is to be social. It's messy and chaotic, yet fun—a mirror of our *actual* lives.

Like when I posted how Chylinski Media sponsored a local men's softball league team. Was that strategic *for business* or was that just a nice *ego* boost for my inner-child for flexing on not 1, but 2 of my exes who played on the team (one from middle school and one from high school)?

Not all social media content needs to be strategic or *by the book*.

It's frustrating how people often default to calling someone an influencer or content creator if they post consistently. Creating content on social is the point of social media... to fucking be social, post and share shit. We're all creators.

Some posts can simply *be*, especially if they make you smile and feel good. I would have missed out on so many interactions on social media if I got caught up in creating a calculated posting plan to get the *best ROI* possible.

I don't follow *the* rules, and *they* don't like that. And for someone who may not know how it feels to be *them*, they can't understand how I can wholeheartedly be me.

My *only* strategy: to continue being me. This looks like posting whenever and wherever I want and focusing on being an expert of myself. That's where and who I want to be.

I've discovered that giving yourself freely *always* comes back to you; I can't hold back. None of this is to brag or to make people think some particular way about me. *I know who I am.* Sharing about how I've found myself through helping others is my way of trying to get you to commit to yourself.

That's a social strategy.

By committing to helping other people, I also committed to myself. That seems like a simple choice for me.

Facts and feelings *always* win.

When using facts in a conversation, no one can question what you're saying. A fact is simply a fact. When using feelings, no one can tell you how to feel. How you feel is valid, and there's nothing anyone can do or say to disprove your feelings. When you're talking about feelings, people might try to give a rebuttal and explain they didn't mean to do whatever it is they did or intend to make you feel what you felt. No matter what their intention was, their actions made you feel a certain way. Whether that was positive or negative, actions affect how you think of others. And it will affect how you choose to respond to their actions.

"Danielle, you make *everyone* seem special," an attendee said to me after a speaking appearance.

I don't think I make anyone seem like anything that they aren't already; I thought to myself. *I help people realize who they already are, and break through the conditioning their past has on them.*

I remember this comment often because I respect the courage it takes for someone to express how they feel.

I feel empowered by sharing my story and experiences, knowing that if *only* a little piece of what I say can help someone along their journey, it can change their life.

I know it can because so many people have changed mine without even knowing it.

I also know how hard it can be for someone to take time out of their professional life or their free time to speak to people. I watched too many speakers come to my college classes and *only* half the students would pay attention, if that. Many would play around on their phone, or disconnect and act like it was a nice break during their day.

When the speaker would ask for questions at the end, so often no one would respond, staring into blank space. These are such missed opportunities when you don't embrace and internalize the mindset that you may learn something that could affect your entire life. The power of storytelling is not fully measurable because you never know the impact you have and how it affects those that may not want to share or ask. The speaker, though, can remember what it felt like to share their experiences, and who was engaged with them.

One of my favorite things whenever I attend a speaking event is to follow the speaker on social media, reach out and thank them. They took the time out of their day to speak with you (as part of an audience). If you reach out, I guarantee you will be part of a tiny percentage and the speaker will remember you for the rest of their career. If you need something, or if your networks or paths end up crossing later, that speaker will remember you as one of the few who reached out. Reaching out to thank someone for their time seems so simple, so easy, and *so obvious*, yet less than two percent of students who have been in my audience have reached out to me. Networking helps not *only* you, but others too.

In November 2020, I spoke about "Working in Sports to Transitioning to a Business Owner," at the University of South Florida. At the end, I concluded with this: "I'm going to tell you something right now that could change your life. And I will also tell you that *only* ten percent of you will do it. I've taken an hour out of my day to volunteer my time to give you advice to help you with your professional career. Please keep me as someone who *you* can reach out to for advice, job opportunities and help. Add me on LinkedIn and let's stay in touch."

The professor who had invited me laughed. "That's so unbelievably true. Thank you so much, Danielle, for giving value and being a resource to these students."

It cost me nothing to share that piece of advice, but for those who didn't connect with me, it could have cost them an opportunity. (Three people out of the class of thirty added me on LinkedIn.) Big #DontWasteMyTime vibes.

I love to help where I can. I've discovered who I am by helping others. From saying yes to speaking appearances to showing coworkers how to set up a calendar invite. From starting a business to having as many meaningful conversations I can. I've built my whole brand, both intentionally and unintentionally, by doing what I can to help.

Anyone can talk about what they want to do, but the execution is the most important. Notice how many people would rather talk about how much work they're doing rather than *actually* do the work. Really, what matters is not how *well* you do it, but *that you try at all.*

You cannot *always* measure the impact you have by speaking about something directly—whether you're speaking to a live audience or posting on social media. You cannot measure or justify everything. Sometimes you want to do *the thing* because you want to do *the thing*. Sometimes you're afraid simply because you're afraid. Understanding whenever you're doing something because you want to makes you feel good or has the potential to make you happy is worth doing.

Do you know how long it took me to walk into a Whole Foods? *That's only for rich people. I know it's a couple of feet walk from my office to grab lunch, but I still don't think I deserve it.*

Seems silly, but this is how debilitating limiting beliefs can be.

My dietitian taught me I deserve to nourish my body, whatever that may look like; the same person who told me to *stop shoulding all over myself.* It wasn't that I *should* go. In fact, I deserve to go. I have the resources and means to go, and by doing so, I'll be able to fuel my body to give all of myself to my work, business and clients, rather than choosing to skip a meal or go somewhere *cheaper.*

Growing up, my dad *always* did the grocery shopping, paying, prepping, and cooking. Big grocery shopping deal guy. He'd travel store to store with his lists and coupons, knowing exactly which items he'd get from each store depending on the sale.

"I'd love some strawberries!" I'd tell my dad when he'd ask what I wanted from the store.

I'd spend the day at school daydreaming about the delicious, fresh strawberries I'd eat when I'd get off the bus. I'd get home and search the fridge, no strawberries.

"Where are the strawberries? I can't seem to find them?"

"Oh, they weren't on sale, so I didn't get them. Maybe next time?"

What the actual fuck?

Little Danielle couldn't wrap her head around not spending a few extra dollars or cents to get me strawberries, but it's what worked best for my dad.

You're talking to a girl whose grandmother (Babcia in Polish, pronounced like bob-she) and grandfather (Dziadek as I mentioned before, pronounced like ja-deck) are straight off the boat from Poland. They came with little money to the United States, and have always treated each penny like it's $1 million.

I remember one time I drove to my Babcia and Dziadek's house. The plan was for me to come over for dinner and get Burger King. *This was after my year of giving up chicken nuggets, LOL.*

My Dziadek showed me all the coupons that he had saved over the years. You read that right, *over the years.* He used to sit down at his kitchen table and cut out the coupons to make sure he saved as much money as he possibly could to continue to gain value over every dollar he had, and by had, I mean earned. Waiting for my Babcia to get home to drive with me to Burger King, my Dziadek proudly held the giant stack of Burger King coupons in his hands.

Yes, a stack big enough needing not one hand, but two.

Once my Babcia got home, I hopped in her car, and her and I drove over. My Dzidaek stayed back. She insisted I go inside to order because she didn't want to order through the drive-thru.

Cue the eye-roll, right? Fine, okay. I can get out of the car and go inside...

Both hands were filled with coupons, not to mention they were all expired, as I'm sure you were already imagining.

My Babcia said, "Make sure you bring back the correct change and the receipt, Danielle."

Now, I was in a position where I had to convince this cashier Burger King man he had to take *ALL* my expired coupons for this meal for 3 people I was about to purchase. I explained I *needed* the coupons to be used, and I *needed* the receipt with the exact change to reflect the coupons. At a quick glance, my Babcia was already doing the math in her head of how much money I was going to be bringing back.

Without a fight, and actually with a big smile, the cashier used *every* coupon for the order... And we couldn't stop laughing during the process. I think it was about *40 chicken nuggets, 6 to 8 sandwiches, and four or five large fries.* LOL.

When we got back to their house, my Dziadek couldn't believe how much food we ordered. He turned to me and said, "You believe this?" in his strong polish accent, pointing to the amount of food spread across the table for just the three of us.

"All under $10," my Babcia said, as she handed him the receipt.

A smile lit up across his face. "Good woman," he said as he put his hand on her shoulder. "Good woman."

So yeah, basically when I go to the grocery store *without* coupons, I feel guilty and totally unprepared. Now, as an adult, too, deciding what's *for me or not for me* when it comes to what I consume is hard. But, I've put in a lot of work to reframe and shape how I can make the best decision for me in the moment, just like I do for my clients.

One time in middle school, I got home from soccer practice and wanted to wear my cleats up the stairs into my bedroom—cleats covered in dirt I just spent over an hour running around in. Mud *actually*. My mom told me I couldn't wear them upstairs.

"But I want to," I said in response.

"I said no."

We went back-and-forth for a few minutes. Eventually, I took them off after choosing not to listen and walking up a few stairs. I went upstairs, grabbed the house phone, ran to my room, closed the door and called the cops.

Yup, 911.

The guy on the other end answered, "9-1-1, what's your emergency?"

I panicked. I was like, *Well, this isn't technically an emergency,* in my head, so I said nothing and hung up.

They called back.

My mom answered.

The police had to come to our house anyway, for precaution—because something *actually serious* could have happened. I hid under my bed the entire time, staring at the cop's shoes. While at the time I didn't think what I was doing was directly measurable, here I am 10+ years later remembering a moment of weakness, feeling out of control, not getting what I wanted. There are many lessons from the story:

1. House phones are dangerous.
2. Decisions have consequences.
3. Don't wear cleats covered in mud on the carpet.

My mom could have hated me, felt so embarrassed she grounded me forever, but instead, she tried to understand my perspective. She realized she told me, "No, you can't walk up the stairs with dirty shoes," but didn't explain to me why I couldn't, or didn't give me a chance to explain why I wanted to. After the craziness and the cops left, she let me explain myself to her.

All I could be was me—my unmeasurable self.

In the end, your people choose you by your actions, thoughts and decisions. They choose whether they want to align with you or walk away.

Your people will find *you* through the small, random comments *you* make, the simple acts of kindness *you* do and the quirky habits that make you *you*. Show the world exactly who *you* are. Focus on being *you*, and people will gravitate towards *you*.

When I go to a new restaurant, I almost *always* try their ranch dressing. Even if I'm not eating a salad, I still order, "Can I get a side of ranch please?" I never know when I'm going to come across my favorite ranch dressing, the one that works best for me, my go-to—kind of like how I never know when my people will find me. There have been a few missed opportunities where I've forgotten to ask or held myself back from asking.

With *every* word, action and decision made publicly, you are subconsciously letting your people find you by creating space for conversation. Instead of worrying about being embarrassed—worry about missing something that was meant for you.

What's the worst that can happen?
Okay, but what's the best-case scenario?

21. Who Are You Choosing?

Audrey, a woman in her late twenties who haaaaaattttted her 9-to-5, eye-rolled these words to me on a business strategy call—"Ugh," she said. "I just want to be you."

Frustrated with herself at the inability to make a bold career move, it seemed easier for her to want to tap out on her own life and "be me" than to figure out what was best for her.

She's choosing me instead of herself? According to her Instagram page, she comes off as confident in herself. Damn.

Naturally, I went on a rant.

"*You are me,*" I said, "in the sense that *everything* I've done, *everything* I feel, *everything* I work towards are things you can do, feelings you can feel, places and people you can connect with. You are choosing day after day to *not* do things that will allow you to have that mentality and approach to life. It's my job to get 'me' out of you, and by 'me,' I mean you. I'm here to help get *you* out of *you*."

Like a placeholder, I represent a version of you until you figure out how to connect to that higher version of yourself.

The idea of *you* versus *you* can be overwhelming. You can't control *everything* that comes into your life, but you can decide what you choose to focus on.

My focus naturally gravitates towards capturing how I feel in each moment, whether it's through pictures, conversations, notes, social posts, captions—you name it. The collection of experiences that make up my life have been so important to me. The idea of showing up online regularly because I wanted to, translated to what we now call a *personal brand*. Choosing myself means doing more of *this*.

Where's your *focus* when choosing yourself?

When I started sharing my experiences, it felt like *not that big of a deal*. Quickly though, I realized others weren't *like me*, when before I thought I was *just like everyone else*.

To some, showing up as yourself is viewed as vulnerable, but for me, it's a non-negotiable. The separation between your work and personal identity sounds scary to some, but to me, having any identity separate from my own has *always* seemed impossible, fake and terrifying to maintain. This is when I learned that work doesn't need to feel like work. And life doesn't need to feel so compartmentalized. It can simply just be.

What makes more sense—showing up as *a version of yourself* or showing up as *you?*

The young girl, not knowing what her focus was entering college, later realized her focus was to simply be herself—by understanding, being and sharing herself with the world.

"You're fully embodying what someone with a Communication—Public Relations major can do with their degree," my dad said to me recently. Until that moment, I hadn't realized just how true that is. And, ironically, I had never made the connection that my dad also has a degree in Communication.

Stop expecting you out of *everybody*, and just focus on who you are.

At the same time, I've learned almost *every* decision that has made me the happiest has been because I trusted my instincts rather than giving others a chance to tell me what was best for me.

"A book is timely. I would never write one." I've heard this so many times.

I'd think to myself; *Are you hung up on the idea that what's being said is then immediately in the past, or are you just too *insert excuse here* to* *follow through on something that you want to do so you tear others down to feel better about yourself?*

I'll just leave that there :)

When you're getting overwhelmed or lost, pause and ask yourself, *what do I want?*

I want to build my business around my life instead of building my life around my business.

Or maybe what do you *not* want?

I don't want there to be a difference between my business and myself. I want to make money by naturally being me.

It's worthwhile to take a step back and think about how you *act in* and *react to* certain conversations.

You know when you're talking away, and then you leave the conversation and your like; *damn:*

I should have said this.

Maybe if I said this instead, the conversation would have ended differently.

If I had mentioned this, they would have reacted differently.

For whatever reason, you valued something more. If you valued what you were complaining about more, you would've done the action and it would've never become a complaint.

Realize who and what type of conversations make you feel powerless, out of control, and not good about yourself—even when you're *trying* so hard to help.

When my clients say things like "I know I *should* have done more," or, "I wish I did this sooner." I remind them they chose not to for a reason. So when you feel your inner dialogue heading in that way, recognize why you didn't *do more.*

"Heyyy!! This event is taking place tomorrow and thought it might be up your alley too! I signed up last night."

Attend a virtual paid event to enhance my business suggested by someone sliding in my LinkedIn DMs who I've never met in person? *I mean, normally I'd say no thanks, but this felt like a sign to say yes and meet other entrepreneurs since, like, I guess I'm one of them now.*

The host started with a series of questions in the chat, asking why we were attending, what we were working on and what we hoped to get out of the event. After each question, she'd read some answers on the live stream. "Awesome, Danielle. You're looking to start a podcast. Yes! I've had one for a while and hosting a podcast is so rewarding. Hopefully, you find the confidence today to take the steps to make it happen."

Did she just read my comment? Whatttttt.

I instantly felt connected to her and the event, more than I thought was possible. *Listen to her podcast,* I wrote in my notes. I had never listened to a podcast before.

The next day, I binged the episodes. She also had published a book and had her book coach on as a guest, sharing how this coach not *only* supported her but also wanted to help share her message with the world. *This is my sign to reach out to this book coach and see if she would be interested in working with me, supporting me in sharing my strong message.*

Feeling bold and a little out-of-body, I emailed the book coach. We planned a time to meet the following week and after 30 minutes of sharing what I wanted to write about, the feedback I received was exactly what I needed to feel confident about moving forward. "The world needs this," the coach said to me. *Validated.*

Two big projects that used to seem so impossible suddenly were right in front of me. Start a podcast and write a book.

In less than a few months, I started the book draft in October 2020, and I launched the podcast, Coffee Date with D, December 2020.

Looking back now; *How was this even possible? Where would I be if I never said yes to this event? Would a podcast exist? Would you be reading this book right now?*

My people found me because *I found myself,* and was comfortable sharing my experiences.

Two years later, Lyla still remembers when I first told her I'd been working on a book. "You know what's crazy? Before I ever messaged you about the virtual event, I knew about you, Chylinski Media, your vibe and what you stood for, but I never had *a reason* to reach out. It wasn't until I saw the women in business event pop up on my LinkedIn feed, when I went with my gut and sent you a message because I genuinely thought you'd love to attend. Little did I know you'd *actually* attend, and we'd become *actual* friends. If you didn't post so damn much on LinkedIn, I probably would not have invited you."

"Wait, woah. That's the entire purpose of this book. What I'm sharing is what I've experienced, *intentionally and unintentionally*. But for whatever reason, I *trusted* what you said because I *trusted* the content I put out about myself and my experiences. I *trusted* the opportunities others subconsciously attracted for me. I *let my people find me*, and I *trusted* them because of how much I *trusted* myself. A true confidence check."

When you take a risk, no matter what the outcome is, you'll be glad you took it. The outcome might be that you learned what not to do, that you ended up having a negative experience that you don't want to repeat, or that you found *exactly* who you're supposed to be, what you're supposed to be doing, or who you're supposed to be doing it with.

22. A Much-Needed Conversation

At the end of my junior year in college, I went to a party with my boyfriend at the time, Noah. A few minutes in, I made eye contact with someone across the yard and I realized it was a student from last summer's orientation.

I walked over to Cooper and said, "Oh my gosh, I cannot believe your freshman year is almost over! It seems like just yesterday I was your Orientation Group Leader!"

Noah saw us standing together, came over before Cooper could even respond, and said something dumb. I can't even remember what it was.

The situation got loud and suddenly friends of both Noah and Cooper were physically holding them back to keep them from *getting into a fight.* Once they went their separate ways, the party carried on for hours after.

Just boy drama; I thought.

Not *everyone* felt the same way.

Later, I called my friend Shay to pick me up. My boyfriend and I said our goodbyes to friends and walked away from the house towards Shay's car at the curb.

A van pulled up at a MPH way over the speed limit and screeched to a stop in front of us. Over six underclassmen jumped out; the *only* face I recognized was Cooper.

One guy, let's call him Toby, began punching my boyfriend as he was getting into the car, pulling him out to the ground, while the other five huddled around and watched.

Then *I was next.*

Toby punched me.

Blood poured down my face, covering my shirt.

"This is what was supposed to happen," Cooper calmly said to Shay, trapped in her car, powerless to the situation unfolding right in front of her eyes.

Shay looked back at him like; *The fuck? 6+ kids jumping two of my friends because she said hi... was supposed to happen?*

The police were called, and I went to the hospital in an ambulance. After waiting for hours in the emergency room, I got five stitches beside my eye and told I had a concussion. Hours later, the hospital cleared me to go home. Since Noah didn't ride in the ambulance with me, he sat in the waiting room for another hour before a nurse called him in.

Noah ended up needing 4 stitches under his eye.

We pressed charges, hoping this would never be able to happen to anyone else; Then, we spent the next year in and out of court.

I was terrified to walk into court, let alone speak, but I did my *best* to stay calm. If there was ever a time to not let fear take over, it was then. And I ended up having to speak on behalf of both myself and my boyfriend.

"Since your boyfriend has a bigger future career than you, it makes sense that you speak up in the moments where either of you technically could," our lawyer told me. "You have less to lose because you have nothing lined up after graduation yet."

Yet, he'd eventually be an Officer in the Military to lead others, but had no problem letting me put my leadership skills to test here instead of his.

All the responsibility fell on me.

This happened right before exam week started. I *only* had one exam, though.

In the immediate aftermath, I emailed my business professor to see if I could reschedule: *Hi Professor, I was in a situation over the weekend where I got punched in the face by a male student off campus and sent to the hospital. I have a minor concussion. Next to my eye, I received five stitches. I'm hoping that I can take my exam at a later date. Please let me know ASAP so I don't have to attempt to study if I can postpone this final exam.*

No reply. So there I was, with a concussion, swollen face, stitches, and bruised eye internally and externally, not being able to wrap my head around the traumatic experience I just had, trying to study for my exam.

I couldn't afford to not pass.

Three days later, I showed up for my exam feeling as prepared as I could be. I waited in line with my bruised, swollen eye. When it was my turn to grab my exam, I put my hand out and looked directly into my professor's soul.

"Oh yeah," he said. "I saw your email. You don't have to take this exam today if you don't want to."

If I didn't want to? Of course I didn't want to. It's not even a matter of not wanting to. I actually really need not to. I'm literally concussed.

"Since I studied the last three days rather than being safe and resting, I want to."

You could have just emailed me back when you saw my email and told me that, instead of knowingly let me suffer.

I knew he could hear my thoughts straight to his core, but it did not faze him.

In this situation, I wasn't able to choose the people who I surrounded myself with or invited into my life. I had to take this course and deal with the professor. But, the experience also showed me I needed to work towards a life where I *could* choose the people who I surrounded myself with.

Not allowing my professor to bully me was on-brand for me, the same way choosing to not respond to my email was on-brand for him.

By choosing myself, I could get through anything.

In a tweet I scrolled by about the 4Ps (product, price, place, and promotion), someone mentioned feeling hypothetically scarred for life because those four words (including elaborate definitions) are so engraved in their head.

I resonated with the *scarred for life statement*, but not for the same reason.

I remember the 4Ps as *trying* to learn these four words and their definitions days after being in the hospital. So when I hear 4Ps, I replay this scenario in my head, scarred for life, *literally*.

Ironic that my current job and lifestyle are literally surrounded by the 4Ps?

Months after the party, two girls reached out and told me they had seen me get punched. When I asked if they would testify on my behalf, they said no.

As a woman, *it's not safe to put yourself in situations you don't need to for someone else,* they say.

I had to fight for myself, flipping my narrative from "this is too scary" to "I have no other option but to speak the truth and hope someone believes me and helps me."

I was the one who had to stare into the mirror *every* day and see the scar on my face. The bruising faded after four-ish months, but the scar will always exist.

I was the one who had to deal with the psychological trauma. I was trying to move past what I had endured the last few months, which at that point felt like my *only* identity. This is a story I've never posted on social media, so I *know* no one realized the impact.

Every time someone says:
Punch
Punch in the face
I wish I could punch them
I want to punch them
... I get silent.

I sort of hold my breath, feeling automatically triggered back to what happened to me. No one notices my reaction; I keep it inside.

I was the one who somehow had to come to peace with my reality if I wanted to move forward, still able to love and trust other people. I had to protect myself physically, mentally, and emotionally.

This was one of the hardest experiences of my life. This was also when I learned how to speak up for myself, no matter how tough a situation felt. Being able to express clear and concise thoughts in the moment felt incredible. The confidence I felt in my voice, even though it was shaking, is something I can't begin to describe. I'm celebrating the *Danielle* who made it through this traumatic event stronger than before.

There was no time to rehearse or practice what I was going to say. There wasn't a narrative I was trying to memorize, or notecards I could rely on when I felt stuck or lost. I had to speak with facts and feelings.

Cooper and his friends had to memorize a narrative from their lawyer in order to get *their story straight.* They were the nervous ones. They were the ones where the judge would think, "I'm surprised you sound so nervous." But to me, it was no surprise; it was clear as day why. They were just like me when I was in that business class trying to talk in front of someone I knew and respected, trying to tell him something I knew was wrong and I didn't fully believe in.

I spoke the truth. I wasn't nervous. They tried to make themselves look and feel better, as if they had done nothing wrong.

For all those times I was hesitant to raise my hand in class, on this day, I chose not to hesitate, but to stand up for myself.

I've learned to speak up and I'm not afraid to do so for others when they can't find their voice in the moment. I had expected my boyfriend at the time to speak up, and it wasn't until *he didn't* that I realized how much power I held. He wasn't able to find his voice—unable to trust the words he spoke would lead to the future that he wanted. So I *had* to.

I didn't have a choice because at the time it was "drop the case because I'm afraid to speak up," or "speak up because I'm afraid what would happen to other women if I didn't." I was fighting for women who cannot find their *strong voice* in a moment where they're *tired* of being strong and just want to be weak *for once*.

At least I'm learning exactly who I am; I thought to myself.

I now recognize that each time I stood up on that podium in court and had to fight for myself, I was learning who I was—as a woman, a daughter, a sister, a friend, a girlfriend, an employee, a business owner, and *everything* else that I am.

My future career mattered then—still matters now, too. That's why I'm at peace sharing this story. Honestly, this experience was a pivotal event in my career. I didn't realize it until I started writing this book. I've *always* been "the strong friend." Early on, I learned when I want to say something, I need to.

I need to speak up.

I spoke up.

I do speak up.

And I will continue to speak up because I've learned you can't wait for someone else to speak up for you.

I was the one who was "*wrong place, wrong time*," they told me. Seemed more like "wrong person, poor judgment" to me. Yet, somehow, the responsibility was on me. No one else.

This is a story that I still continue to process. I've found that sharing parts of my story with people has helped me share the truth and rawness beneath my skin.

Just when I think I can't get any stronger, I'm tested.

"You're so strong." *Yeah, but I don't want to be strong in situations with people who intentionally put me in positions where I have to find, second guess or question my strength.*

I'm worth more than sitting there thinking, *why me?*

Why me didn't matter here, though. I had to just be the *me* I knew best.

Disappointment will happen in your life, and you will have to pick yourself up when it happens. Be prepared. Be ready to use your words in powerful ways. Be confident you'll do what's right. Many fears will come over you in moments when you're scared and feel defeated or helpless. Find it within yourself to allow yourself to push forward.

#DontWasteMyTime coming full force on this one. They could no longer drag me down.

"I want to be a part of your journey with you, not watching from the sidelines," Noah used to tell me.

Well, how's the view from the sidelines?

This experience shaped who I was when I moved out of my parents' house, when I started posting Instagram stories to document my journey in my new apartment, when I received my first job offer through a Facebook DM, when the GM of the Hartford Yard Goats saw my social media and offered me a job, when I had the opportunity to financially and logistically quit my full-time job to work for myself, and when I decided to start writing this book.

Your fear is less than you are, but you're giving it power. Align with it completely; gain leverage to get over the fear by trusting your intuition.

Things are not *always* easy but to *delusionally* take full responsibility for your life? … sounds *worth it* if you ask me.

CONCLUSION: TAKE WHAT YOU NEED, LEAVE WHAT YOU DON'T

I've often seen people mistake impulse for intuition. Making a decision without thinking through the outcome or things that could potentially go wrong? *Impulse.* Or is it intuition? The thing about intuition—You're listening to the voice inside of you with years of experience, aligning with each decision you make, rather than doing something *impulsively out of character.*

Impulse: self-serving, attempting to force control will leave you feeling defensive.

Intuition: self-loving, will leave you feeling good and connected to yourself and others.

When hearing comments from people who couldn't help but to share something out loud with you, it's often hard to decide if it was impulse or intuition speaking. Regardless, the comments made are a reflection of the person making them, not the person they're making them to.

"Miss, how are you drinking? I didn't even think you were 18."

"It's so refreshing talking to someone younger than me, but doesn't seem younger than me."

"I think it's because of your age that you responded that way. Me and my friends who are older do it this way."

while I'm at work "I'd buy you a drink, but I don't think you're old enough."

"Wow, you're really mature for your age. Good for you."

"They're probably older than you. You're def still in college."

Incorrect.

How people act directly correlates to the experiences they've had, what they've been through, how they've learned to handle certain situations, and what they decide to and not to tolerate. It has less to do with age and *everything* to do with their lived experiences.

They don't have the same intuition as you do.

They don't value the same things.

There comes a certain time when age is blurred. You are not ever in a position to comment on someone's actions because of their age, honestly. It's not age or years lived that *matters*, it is experiences—constantly learning and growing, or lack thereof. Using age against people as a tactic to get what you want, a way to make you feel better about yourself and your actions or an excuse to *try* to put someone down... not cool. Insecurity and attempting to show power often shine through with impulse, but can sometimes come off in a low vibe, degrading way.

I fucking love *myself* because I'm *me*.

You deserve to love yourself, too.

You deserve to love yourself because you're *you*.

How are you feeling, *actually?*

What made you say *fuck yeah* or *fuck no* while reading? Pausing to reflect on experiences is something so simple, yet seems like so much time and effort. Yet, reflection and connecting with your intuition can be the missing puzzle piece to full alignment.

I'm here to support you, not judge you. You're here to trust yourself, not question your unapologetic self.

If I was anybody else, I probably would've just stuck to my timeline I set for myself when I first began writing this book. Once I shared with the world what was happening after over a year of writing, the timeline felt extremely tight and locked in. An exhausting pressure to do what *everybody else* wanted me to do, and not let *them* down, was overwhelming. As someone so used to making and keeping promises to others and not letting them down, I was also used to hitting deadlines and never reevaluating them.

I'm going to trust myself, and that's when I began to truly see the power this book was meant to have. It's in letting go of control that you gain absolute control. How it happens is less integral than how it affects you. The purpose of the book was to share stories, but it turned into this weird ass social experiment of realizing that when you fall off from who you are, you can quickly get lost and let other people tell you what you *should* do.

Even when people have your best interest in mind, they can silence your voice and make your project or your goal their own.

What's the gap between your vision and their execution? *You.*

I'm so busy so I didn't have time to trust myself. I thought I was paying someone to help me—essentially as an extension of me.

When you invest in experts, you're paying for their time, intuition and knowledge—not yours. They believe their answers are your answers, which turns into a complete shitshow of miscommunication if you're someone used to trusting your own intuition. But if you're not, you're almost guaranteed to love *their* outcome *for you.* You may *fulfill* what they think is right and you give up *everything* you fundamentally stand for.

Get comfortable setting 1:1 meetings with yourself, like you would for somebody else.

Are you ready to invest in yourself? We can stay up all night doing an assignment for a grade in school for 12+ years, but we can't stay up late to follow our intuition?

"To come out with this current draft, you had to deny your own intuition," a close friend shared with me after reading an old draft of this manuscript and hearing about my writing experience over the last two years. "Which in return has contributed to you feeling like you've spiraled out of actual control. You have, but it's because you fell into the trap of allowing other people's opinions to hold more weight than your own. You made your way out of it though."

Living in your head constantly can cause overthinking; Make your thoughts and emotions concrete by speaking them into existence. You'll probably catch yourself saying; *Wow, that sounds so dumb,* or, *Okay, let's do this.* Rent is expensive nowadays—don't let trash thoughts live rent free.

The irony is one of my favorite parts about doing social media work is when someone comes up to me and says, "Are you doing social for *so-and-so*? I *always* notice your work. When I see your work, I know it's you."

I don't *just* take on any clients and I don't *just* do things to get a paycheck. I'm extremely intentional with whom and where my energy and time goes.

Each second of *your day* is a part of *your life* experience. Life doesn't begin when you're off the clock; it begins the moment you wake up.

I've let go of some of my highest paying clients over the last two years because our values no longer align.

"Just suck it up. That's a lot of money. You don't want to let that go," people would say to me. And I know that. But I'm also worth a lot and when I continuously break myself for people who will never bend for me, the real currency is me, not dollars.

Some call it standards, others call it brand guidelines; for me, it's just *always* been me being *naturally me.* I've been following my intuition for as long as I can remember, and each experience has contributed to the version of myself that I am today. The same way I mentioned we can archive social media posts, we can also archive our memories that have made us *us,* but regardless they have made an impact, and they cannot be erased.

"I wish I met you 20 years ago," someone said to me with a bummed but refreshed look. Comments like this are a reminder of how people are waiting for someone like us to enter their lives.

Sure, people externally won't be able to see your memories or connect the impact, *but you can.* You have the opportunity and the option to allow what you've gone through to intentionally shape you into the person you choose to be.

We often search for the quick fix, or the best way to do something, a how-to guide or the hot new product or trend to make our life *easier,* but the easiest thing we can do is to listen to our intuition—

the constant voice in our head, different versions of ourselves on our shoulders, and our heart-brain connection.

So while some things may seem *delusional*, those that are living in their reality of *delusion* are actually following their natural intuition— something society can never control, *only we can*.

About The Author

DANIELLE CHYLINSKI

*An older sister, millennial, entrepreneur, founder of Chylinski Media,
who learned to live intuitively at a young age*

In January 2020, Danielle founded Chylinski Media to support companies in having a strong online presence that represents their purpose. The business continues to evolve and grow alongside Danielle as a person.

Danielle started her podcast, Coffee Date with D, based on the concept that *you and I* could sit and talk at a coffee shop, but often the conversation is what the coffee shop needs to hear.

Awarded CTNow Best Of Hartford Readers Poll 2019 Best Local Twitter Account @goyardgoats on behalf of the Hartford Yard Goats and Second Runner Up for CTNow Best Of Hartford Readers Poll 2022 Social Media Influencer, Danielle is proud to be born & raised in Connecticut.

Previously, Danielle held the position of Promotions & Marketing Manager for the Hartford Yard Goats, AA Affiliate of the Colorado Rockies and served as Communications Manager at the Alzheimer's Association Connecticut Chapter in Southington, Connecticut, after receiving bachelor's degree in Communication Public Relations with a minor in Integrated Marketing Communications as an honors graduate of Western New England University.

CPSIA information can be obtained
at www.ICGtesting.com
Printed in the USA
JSHW062059160623
43048JS00003B/1